LOOKING
FOR AL

· ·

DIVERSE WRITINGS
FOR THE CURIOUS

Roger Zotti

Visit our website at www.StillwaterPress.com for more information.

First Stillwater River Publications Edition

ISBN-13: 978-1-950339-23-5
ISBN-10: 1-950339-23-8

12345678910

Written by Roger Zotti
Published by Stillwater River Publications, Pawtucket, RI 02860

Publisher's Cataloging-In-Publication Data
(Prepared by The Donohue Group, Inc.)

Names: Zotti, Roger, author.
Title: Looking for Al : diverse writings for the curious / Roger Zotti.
Description: First Stillwater River Publications edition. | Pawtucket, RI :
    Stillwater River Publications, [2019]
Identifiers: ISBN 9781950339242 (hardcover) | ISBN 1950339246 (hard-
    cover) | ISBN 9781950339235 (paperback) | ISBN 1950339238 (paper-
    back)
Subjects: LCSH: Literature--History and criticism. | Authorship. | Motion
    pictures--History and criticism. | Popular culture. | LCGFT: Essays.
Classification: LCC PS3626.O88 L66 2019 | DDC 814/.6--dc23

To Maryann, Tom, Leslie, Katja, Roy, Tee, and Jake

To make a great film you need three things —
the script, the script, and the script.

~Alfred Hitchcock

You taught me language, and my profit on it
Is I know how to curse. The red plague rid you
For learning me your language.

~Caliban,
William Shakespeare's The Tempest

To my mind, that literature is best and most enduring which is
characterized by a noble simplicity.

~Mark Twain

TABLE OF CONTENTS

AUTHOR'S NOTE

Here's my chance to pay tribute to the late William Zinsser, whose *On Writing Well: An Informal Guide to Writing Nonfiction* is the best book I've ever read about writing. Twenty-four invaluable chapters, written by a great writer.

According to him, "We are most of us still prisoners of the lesson pounded into us by the composition teachers of our youth, that every story must have a beginning, a middle, and an end." One of his goals in his book is to help readers/writers escape from that prison.

Take the chapter titled "The Ending." In it, he says when you're ready to end the piece you're writing simply "stop, stop." No summaries. No rehashing. No rounding off. He goes on to write about "the perfect ending," which he believes "should take the reader slightly by surprise.... He didn't expect the article to end so soon, or so abruptly, or to say what it said."

An example of the perfect ending for Mr. Zinsser was how Woody Allen, back in the 1960s, ended one of his stand-up routines. He quotes Allen: "'If people come away relating to me as a person rather than just enjoying my jokes, if they come away wanting to hear me again, no matter what I might talk about, then I'm succeeding.'"

But there's more from Allen! You see, he "does have a problem all his own, unshared by, unrelated to, the rest of America," Zinsser writes. "'I'm obsessed,' Allen says, 'by the fact that my mother genuinely resembles Groucho Marx.' [His remark] is so far out in left field that nobody could see it coming. The surprise that it carries is tremendous. How could it not be the perfect ending?"

TAKE A BOW, MR. HEFLIN

There we were, my friend and I, two teenagers, sitting close to the stage. Nineteen fifty-five was the year, the place New Haven's historic Shubert Theater on a Saturday afternoon.

We were there to see Van Heflin in Arthur Miller's drama *A View from the Bridge*.

What I remember about Heflin's performance as longshoreman Eddie Carbone are his expressive eyes—he acted with them—and his voice, which Derek Sculthorpe says, in his fine, thoroughly researched biography titled *Van Heflin: A Life in Film,* was "one of the best... of any actor of his generation."

Set in the 1950s, the drama involves Eddie, a longshoreman, and his family after two illegal immigrants, Marco (Jack Warden) and Rodolpho (Richard Davalos), cousins of his wife Beatrice (Eileen Heckart), come to live

1

with them and their niece Catherine (Gloria Marlowe), in Brooklyn. They intend to find jobs and become citizens.

When Catherine and Rodolpho fall in love and plan to marry, Eddie becomes delusional and convinces himself Rodolpho is homosexual. Matters are complicated because, we learn, Eddie is possessive of and in love with Catherine, which he won't admit to himself or to anyone else.

While I was reading the Penguin edition of Miller's play, two key scenes brought me back in imagination to that Saturday. The first scene took place early on between Eddie and neighborhood lawyer Alfieri, played by J. Carroll Naish, in the latter's office.

"I'm a patsy, what can a patsy do?" Eddie says to Alfieri. "I mean, in the worst times, in the worst, when there wasn't a ship comin' in the harbor I didn't stand around lookin' for relief …I took out of my own mouth to give to [Catherine]. I took out of my wife's mouth …And now I gotta sit in my own house and look at that a son-of-a-bitch punk [Rodolpho]."

After Eddie leaves Alfieri's office, the lawyer addresses the audience: "I could see every step coming, step after step, like a dark figure walking down a hall toward a certain door."

The second scene occurs near the end of the drama, and in it Alfieri's *dark figure* prophecy comes true. It's the morning of Catherine's wedding to Rodolpho and concludes in the street with Eddie's death as Catherine, Beatrice, Rodolpho, and their neighbors watch.

I see Eddie and Marco fighting. I hear their heavy breathing. I see the knife. I see Marco, the much stronger man, plunge it into Eddie's chest. I see Eddie die.

In a few seconds Alfieri appears and again speaks to the audience: "And so I mourn [Eddie]—I admit it—with a certain alarm."

A moment of silence.

The curtain falls.

Applause.

Separately, the actors return for their bows. Heflin is last, his eyes still ablaze with acting.

WAYNE'S WORLD

John Wayne. Henry Fonda. John Ford. What an intriguing triad!

Wayne was critical of director Ford's award-winning film *The Grapes of Wrath* (1940), which starred Fonda as Tom Joad. As Marc Eliot writes, in his in-depth biography *American Titan: Searching for John Wayne*, the actor believed it was the "prototypical leftist Hollywood film prior to America's entrance into the war...."

Wayne, Ford's longtime friend, also disliked Fonda because his "real-life politics seemed too close to Tom Joad's." Aware of Wayne's reaction to the movie, Fonda "dismissed [him] as just one big, dumb actor without a political thought in his head or an ounce of discernible talent."

Eliot says Ford regarded Fonda and Wayne as "his two favorite sons," and believed "Fonda's acting style is driven by aggressive narcissism, Wayne's by soft-spoken narcissism." Of the two actors, Ford leaned toward Fonda as the better one, "but it wasn't much of a tilt. He still liked Wayne as the best projection of himself on-screen but didn't think either actor was that good on his own, and if they gave great performances in his films, it was because he brought it out of them."

Thirty-four years old, married and the sole support of his family, Wayne didn't serve in the U.S. military supposedly because of "family dependency reasons," Eliot writes. Also, Wayne claimed he had an injured shoulder, "though it didn't bother him much when he was working [early in his career] as a stuntman or riding horses or throwing punches."

Enter Herbert J. Yates, the head of Republic Studios. Wayne had made several financially successful films for him, and he helped the actor avoid military service by having his lawyers prove he was more valuable to America making movies than serving in the military.

Over the years Wayne, for better or for worse, established himself as a super patriot. One reason for his excessive patriotism was, as the actor's third wife Pilar told Ford's grandson Dan, his attempt to atone for avoiding the draft.

According to Eliot, a "gray cloud" also followed Fonda after the war "for his lifelong liberalism, and his too real and impassioned portrayal of Tom Joad in *The Grapes of Wrath*."

Ultra-conservative Darryl F. Zanuck, head of Twentieth Century Fox, didn't want Fonda cast as Wyatt Earp in Ford's forthcoming *My Darling Clementine* (1946). Instead, he wanted Wayne for the role, but Ford insisted on Fonda, one reason being the director's respect for military veterans: Fonda had served with distinction for three years in the Navy and was awarded the Naval Presidential Unit Citation and the Bronze Star.

Zanuck relented. Fonda portrayed Earp.

Despite his intolerance of people who disagreed with his politics, Wayne was often forgiving. Larry Parks, who was Jewish, was critically and commercially lauded for his performances in *The Jolson Story* (1946) and several years later in *Jolson Sings Again*, "…despite the large number of studio heads who were Jewish," Eliot writes, "Jews were rarely portrayed on-screen. Parks's performances were considered breakthroughs."

In 1951 the House on Un-American Activities Committee subpoenaed Parks, who admitted he had been a member of the Communist Party. He "begged not to have to name names of those others who were fellow members," Eliot writes.

He caved in, however, and named names, and didn't work in films for ten years.

Eliot quotes Wayne: "'…too bad Larry had been a Communist, but damn courageous of him to admit it. Young Parks needs our moral support. He should be commended for being a good patriotic American…. When any member of the Party breaks with them, we must welcome him back into American society. We should give him friendship and help him find work again in our industry.'"

Feared by many in the film industry because she seemed to know everything about everyone—and what she didn't know she invented—Hollywood gossip columnist Hedda Hopper responded by unmercifully criticizing Parks and bashing Wayne, president of the Screen Actors Guild at the time, for "[his] nonservice in the military."

JIMMY'S WAY

Jimmy Cannon's *Nobody Asked Me, But... The World of Jimmy Cannon* is a collection of the columnist's diverse writings from the forties to the seventies. Edited by Tom and Jack Cannon, Cannon's nephews, it proves that Jonathan Yardley, writing for *Sports Illustrated*, was correct when he said Cannon "ranks with Ring Lardner and Red Smith among writers who changed the face of the sports page."

Cannon is at his strongest when he writes about middleweight champion Tony Zale's first fight against top ranked contender Rocky Graziano, at Yankee Stadium, on September 27, 1946. (They were to fight two more times.)

The challenger was favored to win because he was several years younger than Zale and had flattened seven straight opponents. Also most boxing scribes believed the champion was past his prime.

Zale proved the experts wrong: Before 39,827 fans he came from behind to retain his title with a devastating sixth round knockout of Graziano.

What happened in Zale's dressing room after the fight was as startling as his victory. Cannon writes, "[Zale] was like a man who had been dozing in the sun [and] avoided conversation because it might disturb his mood." Bombarded with questions by reporters, he gave the same answer to every question he was asked.

It took a while but a reporter, at first unable to believe what he heard and saw, bellowed, "This guy's knocked out."

Zale's handlers swung into action. They held their man under the shower for a long time and he eventually regained consciousness.

"Graziano," Cannon writes, "had knocked him out, but his body obeyed the instructions in his mind and he had refused to fall down. He had punched because that is what a fighter is supposed to do. That is what they pay him to do. It did not occur to Zale that this was unusual. You are sent in there to fight and that is what you do as long as you can do it, no matter what happens to you."

KIDS WRITE THE BEST THINGS

*"People sometimes look surprised when I say that
I love to get fan letters from children.
I'm surprised that they're surprised."*

~*Ursula Le Guin*
No Time to Spare

Attention readers with humanistic and active imaginations: You'll appreciate what Ursula Le Guin says about the mail she receives from young children. In her essay called "Kids' Letters," from her book *No Time to Spare: Thinking About What Matters*, she writes: "Computer spell-checking takes all the flavor out of nonprescriptive, creative spelling that can give delight to the reader."

Some examples: "favrit pert... favroit prt... faevit pairt... favf pont."

The author of novels, short stories, poems and essays, Le Guin loved to read letters and novels kids under ten send to her. Their novels are usually fifty words long," she says. Her next step is to "answer these letters at least by thanking every child by name. I can't usually do much more than that."

She had faith in the creative power of young children, especially "when teachers let the kids write whatever they want, if they want to write anything, it works."

Adult control! Be wary of it because it "inevitably takes [away] the wild unpredictability of stories and pictures that come straight from each child's imagination. Such illustrations, stories, and booklets give me almost unalloyed delight." As for computers, Le Guin writes, "[It] may make writing easier, but that's not always an advantage: ease induces haste and glibness." Spot on!

And those kids who write books "should be proud," she writes. "And at the end, they all write 'The End' with a proud flourish. Their teacher is proud of them. I am proud of them. I hope their family is proud of them. To have written a book is a very cool thing, when you are six or eight or ten years old. It leads to other cool things, such as fearless reading. Why would anyone who has written a book be afraid of reading one?"

~~~

"... let the kids write whatever they want."

Do you hear that, teachers and parents? And if there are any school administrators out there reading this essay, pay attention to Le Guin's words. (Even if she doesn't have a teaching certificate, so what? That might be an advantage. Her sage advice is all that counts.)

"...the wild unpredictability of stories and pictures that come straight from each child's imagination..."

Administrators, teachers, and parents, your job is to treasure and preserve a child's unpredictability. Don't stifle it. Don't fear it. Encourage it! I say this because my classroom experience has led me to believe unpredictability isn't appreciated by most educators.

Why isn't it appreciated? There are many reasons. Four are: Too many teachers are narrow minded, too obey-the-rules conscious, afraid of what isn't planned, and often overly formally educated.

Imagine how great it would be if your kids had Ursula Le Guin for their teacher!

CAPITAL PUNISHMENT OR NOT

Date: **March 25, 2015**

Setting: **Madison Square Garden**

Event: **The New York Rangers vs. Washington Capitals. (Washington won, 3-1.)**

Seated in front of us was acclaimed actor and director Tim Robbins, probably best remembered for his portrayal of Andy Dufresne in 1994's *The Shawshank Redemption*, and for his Oscar winning performance in a supporting role as Dave Boyle in 2003's *Mystic River*.

As a director his best effort is *Dead Man Walking* (1995). Based on Sister Helen Prejean's 1993 book of the same title, the movie is about her opposition and inner conflict regarding capital punishment. She knows Matthew Poncelet, the young man on death row whom she counsels and befriends, has few redeeming qualities. As the murderer of two recent high school graduates, his attitude about his crime tests her belief in the sacredness of every human being.

Though director Robbins's opposition to capital punishment is strong, he doesn't hedge when it comes to the horrific pain the murdered young women's grieving parents endure, nor does he offer any excuses for the defiant, swaggering, remorseless Poncelet, played with total believability by Sean Penn.

Under Robbins's direction there are also exceptional performances from Susan Sarandon, who as Sister Helen won 1995's Oscar for Best Actress; from Raymond J. Barry and R. Lee Ermey, two fine character actors who portray the victims' fathers; and from Roberta Maxwell as Poncelet's mother Lucille, a broken woman wracked with guilt and pain over her son's actions.

Sister Helen's book challenges readers to reflect on what Albert Camus writes in "Reflections on the Guillotine," from his book of essays *Resistance, Rebellion, and Death*, about "no government [being] ever innocent enough or wise enough to lay claims to so absolute a power as death."

Opponents of capital punishment must ask her how she'd feel if someone in her family was murdered. Would she still be against the death penalty? In her book she answers the question: "I am acutely aware that my beliefs about the death penalty have never been tested by personal loss. Let Mama or my sister, Mary Ann, or my brother, Louie, be brutally murdered and then see how much compassion I have…. No one has shot my loved ones in the back of the head."

THE LONDON UNDERGROUND

A key scene in *Darkest Hour,* the film in which Gary Oldman transformed himself into an energetic Winston S. Churchill to win 2018's Oscar for Best Actor, takes place on the London Underground.

"Have you never seen a Prime Minister ride the London Underground before?" Churchill says to the astonished riders, who then begin laughing.

"How are you all bearing up? Good spirits?" Churchill continues. "Let me ask you something that's been weighing on my mind. Perhaps you can provide me with an answer. You, the British people — what is your mood? Is it confident? If the worst is to come to task, and were the enemy to appear on those streets above, what would you do?"

The riders' responses are loud and clear: **Fight... Fight the fascists.... Fight 'em with anything we can lay our hands on... They'll never take Piccadilly.**

"What if I put it to you all that we might, if we ask nicely, get very favorable terms from Mr. Hitler, if we enter into a peace deal right now," he says. "What would you say to that?"

The passengers respond:

Never!

Never!

Never!

Never!

Never!

Approaching a young boy, perhaps eleven or twelve, seated with his mother, Churchill asks, "Will you never give up?" and the youngster boldly replies: *No! Never!*

Even if the scene never happened, Anthony McCarten, who wrote the book *Darkest Hour* and screenplay, and the film's director Joe Wright use dramatic truth to make the audience believe it happened.

In McCarten's book he does the same thing by speculating how an important talk between Churchill and Lord Halifax went:

Winston: Viscount Halifax, as I said yesterday, the approach you propose is not only futile, but involves us in a deadly danger.

Halifax: THE DEADLY DANGER HERE IS THIS ROMANTIC FANTASY OF FIGHTING TO THE END!!!

What *is* the 'end' if not the destruction of all? There is nothing even remotely patriotic in death or glory if the odds are on the former; nothing inglorious in trying to shorten a war that we are clearly losing.

Winston: Europe is still....

Halifax (*cutting him off*): EUROPE IS LOST! Lost. And before our forces are wiped out completely, this is the time to negotiate in order to obtain the best conditions possible. It would not be in Hitler's interest to insist on outrageous terms. He will know his own weaknesses. He will be reasonable.

Churchill (*unable to bear this talk*): When will the lesson be learned? How many more dictators must be wooed, appeased — good God, given the immense privileges — before we learn... that you can't reason with a tiger when your head is in its mouth!

Dramatic truth. Speculation. Director's license. *Sometimes* when the legend becomes fact, as we're told in John Ford's movie *The Man Who Shot Liberty Valance* (1962), use the legend.

IN THIS CORNER—THE PIG BABY

The dream child moving through a land
Of wonders wild and new,
In friendly chat with bird or beast—
And half believe it true.

Lewis Carroll
~Alice's Adventures in Wonderland

'm puzzled why Lewis Carroll wanted to end his novel *Alice's Adventures in Wonderland* on a happy note. In the last chapter, Alice's older sister tells the reader "she pictured to herself how this little sister of hers would, in the after-time, be herself a grown woman; and how she would keep, through all her riper years, the simple and loving heart of her childhood; and how she would gather about her other little children, and make *their* eyes bright and eager with many a strange tale...."

A nice ending for kids but not for adults. It's difficult to envision the adult Alice with her *bright and eager* eyes telling little children stories, strange or otherwise, because most of the seven-year-old Alice's adventures in Wonderland are nightmares. As a character in Mark Z. Danielewski's novel *House and Leaves* says, "No one ever really gets used to nightmares."

~~~

Hard to believe that most children—even those who aren't named Alice—would follow a rabbit down a hole in the ground, especially a rabbit that took a watch from its pocket and looked at it.

Though she "had never before seen a rabbit with either a waistcoat-pocket, or a watch to take out of it," Carroll writes, she followed the rabbit down the rabbit hole—which I'm sure we've all wanted to do when we were children—and "never once [considered] how in the world she was to get out again."

And Alice begins

FALLING!

"Either the well was very deep, or she fell very slowly, for she had plenty of time as she went down to look about her, and to wonder what was to happen next," writes Carroll.

What Alice soon experiences is her most disturbing nightmare, which is meeting the frightening and mad

Duchess who tosses a baby in her direction, but with the quick reflexes of youth, Alice catches the infant.

She looks at it and what she sees disturbs her: "The poor little thing was snorting like a steam engine," Carroll writes, "and kept doubling itself up and straightening itself out again." Alice knows she must protect the child from the Duchess's lunacy, that "If I don't take this child away with me, they're sure to kill it in a day or two."

Hurrying outside with the infant, she hears it grunt, looks at its face, and sees its nose looks "much more like a snout than a real nose."

After putting the "little creature down," to Alice's relief it trots away into the woods. Had it grown up, Alice believes, "it would have made a dreadfully ugly child, but it makes a rather handsome pig." Then she muses about "other children she knew who might do very well as pigs...."

I'm sure you remember the grinning Cheshire Cat, who made an appearance in the Mad Duchess scene; and if you don't, shame on you. Well, it's back and still grinning. In the book's most memorable conversation, Alice asks it for directions:

The Cat: That depends a good deal on where you want to get to.

Alice: I don't care much where —

The Cat: Then it doesn't matter which way you go.

Alice: —so long as I get *somewhere*.

The Cat: Oh, you're sure to do that, if you only walk long enough.

Alice: What sort of people live about here?

The Cat: In that direction lives a Hatter: and in that direction lives a March Hare. Visit either.... They're both mad.

Alice: But I don't want to go among mad people.

The Cat: Oh, you can't help that. We're all mad here. I'm mad. You're mad.

Alice: How do you know I'm mad?

The Cat: You must be, or you wouldn't have come here.

When the Cat asks about the baby, Alice says, "'It turned into a pig,'" and the Cat replies, "'I thought it would.'"

An angry Alice criticizes the Cat for "appearing and vanishing so suddenly," but before she can say anything else, it begins disappearing again, "this time... quite slowly, beginning with the end of the tail, and ending with a grin, which remained sometime after the rest of it had gone."

"Well! I've often seen a cat without a grin," Alice thinks, "but a grin without a cat! It's the most curious thing I ever saw in my life!"

"SHARED UNDERSTANDING"

Granted, the heart of Candace Millard's latest book, *Hero of the Empire: The Boer War, A Daring Escape, and the Making of Winston Churchill*, is Churchill's incredible escape from a Boer prison in 1899. At the same time, books that shaped the lives of famous people are crucial to understanding them, which is why in Millard's masterly written work I concentrated on the influential books Churchill read.

As a youngster Churchill entered St. James, a private school in London, and his two years there were a nightmare. He found the school, Millard writes, "a grim, joyless, struggle, and himself more often than not at the bottom of his classes." Nor was he well-liked by his classmates.

As for his parents, they "all but abandoned him, so he was left with few places to run for solace and friendship."

Turning to books as a refuge, one of his lifelong favorites was Robert Louis Stevenson's *Treasure Island*, which his father gave to him when he was nine and a half years old. "I remember the delight with which I devoured it," he writes in his memoir *The Early Years: 1874-1904*, adding that "My teachers saw me at once backward and precocious, reading books beyond my years and yet at the bottom of the form."

For Churchill, becoming lost in books was the most pleasant memory of his years at St. James and the beginning of a lifetime of reading.

Fast forward to 1899 and his escape from the Boer prison. Enter John Howard, a mining manager who met Churchill in Witbank, a mining town in South Africa. An Englishman, he lived in Transvaal, the Boers trusted him, and he even became a naturalized citizen of South Africa.

He gave Churchill *Kidnapped*, another Stevenson novel.

He gave Churchill asylum, too, though he was aware if he were caught hiding a fugitive, he'd be tried for treason and shot.

The book saved Churchill's sanity. On its pages he "found something more than refuge or even knowledge," Millard writes. "He found shared understanding." Through [seventeen-year-old David Balfour, the novel's main character], "Stevenson expressed the same feelings of foreboding, powerlessness, and shame with which Churchill was struggling as he sat alone in Howard's office."

Stevenson's novels, Churchill writes in his memoir, "awakened sensations in which I was only too familiar. To be a fugitive, to be a hunted man is a mental experience by itself. The risks of the battlefield, the hazards of the bullet or the shell are one thing. Having police after you is another. The need for concealment and deception breeds an actual sense of guilt very undermining to morale."

ALL BROTHERS

Joyce Carol Oates's insightful and bold book *On Boxing* delivers a fresh take on the sweet science. The book is a tribute to prizefighters, she writes, "who fight one another with only their fists and their cunning who are all contemporaries, all brothers, belonging to no historical time."

Oates became aware of the pain boxers inflict on each other when she was twelve years old. Her father took her to a Golden Gloves tournament in Buffalo, New York, and she asked him why the boys were fighting and why they wanted to hurt each other.

"Boxers don't feel pain quite the way we do," was his reply.

She echoes her father's words when she writes that boxing is a matter of "being able to move through pain to victory. I believe that's the boxer's hope."

To prove her point she quotes heavyweight champion Gene Tunney: "'Harry Greb gave me a terrible whipping....The referee, the ring itself, was full of blood....'" Though it was during that first fight with Greb that Tunney lost his light-heavyweight title, he says, "I knew I had found a way to beat Harry eventually.'"

Tunney adds: "'If boxing in those days had been afflicted with the Commission doctors we have today—who are always poking their noses into the ring and examining superficial wounds—the first fight with Greb would have been stopped before I learned how to beat him. It's possible, even probable, that if this had happened I would never have been heard of again.'"

One of America's most prolific and important fiction writers, Oates, in *On Boxing*, evaluates several authors who have written about the sweet science. She slams A.J. Liebling's book *The Sweet Science: Boxing and Boxiana—a Ringside View*, which is regarded as a classic. It's "a peculiarly self-conscious assemblage of pieces," she writes, "arch, broad in its humor, rather like situation comedies in which boxers are 'characters' depicted for our amusement."

While she extols W.C. Heinz, Norman Mailer, Ted Hoagland, Budd Schulberg, John Schulian, George Plimpton, and Hugh McIlvanney, her highest praise is reserved for Leonard Gardner, the author of *Fat City*: His novel is "less about boxing than about the strategies of self-deception; a handbook of sorts in failure, in which boxing functions as the natural activity of men totally unequipped to comprehend life. The boxers of Gardner's Stockton,

California—that notorious fight town—seem to exist in a world as claustrophobic as a training gym...."

Gardner's book digs into "the underside of the American dream, in which men with some minimal skill in a dangerous sport are hired to fight one another for pitifully small purses: it is a measure of the novel's irony that victory, for such stakes, is hardly to be distinguished from failure." He has the gift of "realizing, as if from the inside, the psychology of the man born to fight, the man who knows nothing but fighting, no matter the suicidal nature of his calling."

MICKEY WOULD LOVE YOUR TITLE

In the mid-fifties, when I was a junior in high school, our English class was reading Charles Dickens's *David Copper-field*. After reading thirteen pages I quit, but I magically faked my way through class discussions by being quiet, by never volunteering, by becoming almost invisible. (Shades of Claude Rains.)

When we were assigned what our English teacher Mr. Herman Stubb called a critical appreciation of Dickens's book, I wrote a paper instead on Mickey Spillane's *Kiss Me Deadly*, which I read in two days.

My reasoning: That previous summer I saw the movie version of the book. Ralph Meeker played Mickey's private eye Mike Hammer. (For Spillane, in his novels Hammer was a hero; for the folks who made the movie, Hammer was trans-formed into a thug who, thanks to Meeker's performance, was more thuggish than the movie's thugs.) I loved it. Meeker was sensational. So why not read the book and write about it?

I wasn't surprised that my grade for the Dickens paper, which I didn't write, was **F**. What surprised and disappointed me was the absence of any comments about my Spillane effort which I titled, by the way, *Kiss My Ass Gently*.

Anyway, two of my classmates thought it was a great title. I did too. I still do.

One afternoon, after class, I approached Mr. Stubb, who read my mind and said, after taking a seat behind his desk and rubbing his chin, "The assignment, young man, was to write a paper on *David Copperfield*."

Ask him! Ask him! "Did you ever read *Kiss Me, Deadly*, Mr. Stubb, or see the movie?"

His response: "Trash!"

Suddenly I had what Mr. Stubb, early in the year, called a moment of epiphany, a word I never heard before. I recall he said the best examples of epiphanies are found in a book of short stories by—I think the author's name was Joyce and she came from Ireland. He said the word epiphany had religious implications and then explained what it was.

(After I graduated from high school, I didn't keep in touch with Mr. Stubb, but friends told me he stayed two more years at the school, then went elsewhere.)

Anyway, back to that day. "Mr. Stubb," I stammered. "Mr. Stubb, listen, please, to the way Spillane begins *Kiss Me Deadly*."

And I was out of breadth when I finished reading it to him.

"I am very impressed with your memory," he said, "but if you want to impress someone with a quotation from a book, do not memorize its opening sentences. No. Memorize the book's last several sentences. *Moby Dick* ends this way: 'It was the devious-cruising Rachel, that in her retracing search after her missing children, found another orphan,' and Fitzgerald's *The Great Gatsby*, my favorite American novel, ends with a touch of lyricism from its narrator Nick Carraway: 'So we bear on, boats against the current, borne back ceaselessly into the past.'"

He paused, as if to admire what he had said.

I am not exaggerating when I say I have no problem recalling that day so many years ago, of remembering Mr. Stubb's various facial expressions and voice, of his quick look over my shoulder to make sure no one was in earshot, and of what he said to me: "Your pal Spillane writes trash. Trash! But, young man, it is good trash. Very good. And your Spillane paper was good, too, and I know Mickey would love its title."

SNARKS ARE LIKE THAT SOMETIMES

"[The Boojum] looks like nothing else on earth."

~Joseph Wood Krutch
The Forgotten Peninsula

A Poem

In *Masterpiece Mystery*'s *Lewis* — it's the episode titled "The Soul of Genius" — street smart Inspector Robbie Lewis and his partner, the cerebral Sergeant James Hathaway, are searching a suspect's house for clues. The doorbell rings. A package is delivered. Lewis unwraps it and reads aloud from the card inside. "Gracie books... *The Hunting of the Snark: An Agony in Eight Fits*. Original working manuscript. Annotated by Lewis Carroll. Dated January 1876."

The university educated Hathaway is astounded. "I studied this," he says. "This is incredible."

Lewis: Studied it? I thought it was a poem.

Hathaway: It's a profoundly theological piece of work. It's theological and philosophical. It's about a ten man crew in search of a Snark.

Lewis: And what's a Snark?

Hathaway: Precisely the question everyone asks.

"People don't really know what a snark is, or what they're searching for," Lewis says, with a hint of skepticism. Hathaway agrees adding that though nobody knows what a snark looks like, "the danger in finding it [is that the finder] will softly, suddenly vanish away. It's about the search for meaning, being and nothingness, the unanswerable questions of existence."

The Baker

One of the Snark searchers is the Baker, whom Carroll describes as forgetful and possessing an "ungainly" appearance, his "intellect small." But he's courageous, however, "And that, after all, / is the thing one needs with a snark."

In "Fit the Third" the Baker tells a "sad story" his uncle once told him that concludes like this: "…beware of the day, / If your Snark be a Boojum! For then / You will softly and suddenly vanish away, / And never be met with again." Shattered and haunted by his uncle's words, the Baker now lives in a state of dread — the dread of annihilation — because he knows what will happen if he were to encounter a Snark who is a Boojum.

It's a "notion," he says, "I cannot endure."

In "Fit the Eighth, The Vanishing," the Snark travelers have landed on an island. Later in the day they're (almost) overjoyed when they realize the Baker—the Butcher calls him "a desperate wag"—is missing. Apparently he has seen a Snark and set out to capture it.

The travelers wait and listen: "Some fancied they heard in the air / A weary and wandering sigh / That sounded like '—jum' but the others declare / It was only a breeze that went by." Give the travelers credit because "They hunted till darkness came on, but they found/ Not a button, feather, or mark." Finally, they admit the Baker "had softly and suddenly vanished away— / For the Snark was a Boojum, you see."

The Meaning

Lewis Carroll's poem, *The Hunting of the Snark* (published April 1, 1876), is **Sinister Bizarre Surreal**. Some readers and critics have called it a nonsense poem. So what? Stick with it! Ponder it! After enough pondering it makes sense, sort of.

(Or maybe have fun with it. Let it resonate in your imagination, then give it all kinds of meanings, and I guarantee each time you read the poem it'll have a different meaning.)

Since its publication critics have differed widely about what the poem means. Fortunately, the author shed some light on that problem. To a nineteen-year-old woman who had read the poem a year or two after its publication and, like most readers, was bewildered by it, Carroll writes:

"I have a letter from you asking me 'Why don't you explain the Snark?' [It's] a question I ought to have answered long ago.'"

But Carroll says he can't: "Are you able to explain things that you don't yourself understand?"

SAVED

That Michael Kitchen is an exceptionally versatile actor is proved by contrasting his Deputy Superintendent Christopher Foyle character of the British series *Foyle's War* with his Greg Brentwood character of *Alibi* (2008), a superb English made-for-television movie.

The first episode of *Foyle's War* ("The German Woman") is set in the town of Sussex during World War II. A local magistrate's Austrian wife is found murdered. Painted on a tree near her dead body is a swastika.

When we're first introduced to the unflappable Foyle, he's meeting with Assistant Commissioner Summers (Edward Fox), in the latter's office. There he makes it clear to Summers he wants a transfer. He's wasting his time, he says, investigating local crimes.

Refusing his request, Summers says, "You know, Foyle, if you weren't so damn obstinate, you'd see I'm actually on your side. You do a good job. No telling where you might be once the war is over."

Foyle's response: "It'll depend on who wins, I suppose."

Summers changes his mind and assigns Foyle to investigate the murder of the official's wife. Not surprisingly, he solves the case.

Turning to *Alibi*, Greg is giving his wife Linda (Phyllis Logan) an extravagant nineteenth anniversary party at their home. After the party he fights with and kills Martin Shaps, his business partner and Linda's lover. A civil servant named Marcey Burgess (the great Sophie Okonedo), moonlighting as a waitress, discovers Greg standing over Shaps's body and helps him dispose of it.

An early sign Greg might unravel occurs at his home the evening after Martin's death. He and Linda are questioned by two police officers. The older officer tells him, kindly, he doesn't expect his "recall to be one hundred percent, but I wouldn't be nagging you if it wasn't so vital. You with me?"

He reminds Greg that he and his wife were "the last people to see Martin alive." When the officer asks if Martin showed up with anyone, Greg's answers are rapid. Hard to follow: "Well to be honest when I opened the door a bunch of them were together—and I got a thousand things on my mind cuz I've been trying to organize this for months—a big surprise—a massive surprise—to thank her for all those glorious years—nineteen glorious years—matter of fact—so I couldn't say who came with who or whom. Whom? Hmm."

As for Okonedo's Marcey, she has become involved in a dangerous and exciting situation. Calm and confident, whip-smart, she enjoys the challenge of stepping outside her safe, dull life to deviously outmaneuver the authorities.

(One has to wonder if she *always* possessed the talent to outfox people but never had the opportunity to use it. But maybe that's another story for another time.)

Near the end of the movie it's clear Greg won't become unhinged because, like Marcey, he's enjoying himself. After all, he has gotten away with a serious crime and met an interesting young woman who saved his ass.

LOOKING FOR AL

All I know is, if you're alive, everything is enriching.

~Al Pacino

Reading and Acting

*A*l Pacino, in Conversation with Lawrence Grobel* is a book of revealing, discerning, and often humorous interviews that took place with the Oscar winning actor between 1979 and 2005.

Early on, Pacino tells Grobel he "was brought up on many different writers, from Balzac to Shakespeare. I know I came from the [New York] streets and had no formal education, but I read this stuff, and it's the Russians that I really felt." He read Anton Chekov, who Pacino believes was crucial to his development as an actor. He read Turgenev. He read Fyodor Dostoyevsky and says if he could choose a writer to pen his biography, it would be him, "though he's not a lot of laughs."

Those writers gave him a purpose in life. "[They] got me through my twenties," he says.

"Can you get to a point in acting where you feel you're not acting?" Grobel asks, and Pacino says, "That's what you try to do the whole time—to get to a point where it's instinctive. [What] you really try to learn is how *not* to act. That's where it's at. Acting is *not* acting." (In a later interview Pacino contradicts himself—and good for him. He tells Grobel he isn't sure how to define acting. "[It's] still a mystery to me," he says. "You never understand it. You can rehearse… but the actual acting, I still don't get it.")

Grobel asks: Do "you see yourself as a stage actor who makes movies more than a film actor who also does plays?"

Pacino responds: "I don't consider myself one or the other," though he favors "the theater simply because it's the life I was most familiar with…" The theater was what "attracted me to being an actor, where I feel the most like I am enjoying the lifestyle of it [and] when I do go onstage, that's where I belong."

Before 1972's *Godfather*, Pacino says he was "a gypsy," homeless, penniless, living "in dives and dumps, in rooming houses," where paradise "was anything that had running water and a bathroom in the room…" But after the first *Godfather*, Pacino was famous. Then came *Serpico*, *The Godfather II*, *Dog Day Afternoon*, and … *and Justice for All*, and he found himself more in demand.

Initially he had trouble handling his celebrity, but he remedied the problem by returning to the stage. "It was my way of dealing with the success I had, my way of coping," he says. "It was a way of escaping the responsibility of what was happening."

On Shakespeare's *Richard III*

In *Looking for Richard* (1996), Grobel says, "You're out there interviewing street bums and Oxford scholars, you're swinging on a swing wearing a baseball cap backward and reciting monologues, you're setting off alarms in Shakespeare's bedroom in Stratford, you're sitting around a table with Kevin Spacey and Penny Allen arguing how to play a scene, you're in costume seducing Winona Ryder, sending Alec Baldwin to the tower, screaming for your horse. People are going to have to be prepared for that—it's unlike anything they might expect."

"Everybody's always interpreting [Shakespeare] in different ways," Pacino replies. "This is another way," adding his *Richard III* isn't the whole drama but simply a "taste.... Maybe that's what it should be called: *A Taste of Richard*. The person who sees this picture and enjoys it is the person who has a respect for Shakespeare but is afraid of Shakespeare."

Looking for Richard was, he continues, "...entertainment... It's a jaunt... jubilant. I enjoy the humor of it; the things that happen spontaneously on the street are very funny."

One of those marvelous street scenes occurs when Pacino, a turned around baseball cap on his head and wearing old clothes, is walking the New York streets interviewing everyday people, not Shakespearean actors or scholars. For film critic Jack Garner of *Gannett News Service*, in his review of the movie, the most memorable interview involves "a homeless man in Manhattan [who] astutely observes that a knowledge of Shakespeare teaches people how to communicate with words 'instead of guns.'"

In *Life on the Wire: The Life and Art of Al Pacino*, Andrew Yule points out the actor knew he was taking risks with his 1979 Broadway *Richard III* and his 1996 *Looking for Richard* movie. Big risks.

But Pacino wasn't deterred and relished the perils that making the stage play and the movie involved. "The thing is in *doing* it," he said, "*that's* what it's all about. Not in the results of it. After all, what *is* a risk? It's a risk *not* to take risks. Otherwise, you can go stale and repeat yourself…. Anybody who cares about what he does takes risks."

Is *Looking for Richard*, Grobel asks, an "Al Pacino as you've never seen him before," and the actor replies, "I hope every part I play is as-you've-never-seen-me from the last part I played."

THE WILL O' THE WISP AND THE TIGER

*O*nce *They Heard the Cheers* (1979), W.C. Heinz's compilation of interviews with nineteen athletes, proves why he was an outstanding writer of literary nonfiction who wrote mainly about sports.

Take his interview with Middletown, Connecticut's Willie Pep. The former featherweight champion talked about the time he was fighting "a tall black guy from the Salem AC named Ray Roberts." The place was Norwich CT, the year 1937, and both Pep and his opponent were amateurs at the time. Outweighed by twenty-plus pounds, Willie lost the three-round decision.

Pep turned pro in 1940, his foot and hand speed soon earning him the nickname the "Will o' the Wisp." In 1945 he won the National Boxing Association featherweight championship by defeating Sal Bartolo. Considered one of the best defensive fighters of all time, he compiled an amazing

229-11-1 record. Three of his losses were to Sandy Saddler, one of the greatest featherweight champions ever.

Their fourth Sadler-Pep fight took place on September 26, 1951, and "was one of the roughest, toughest bouts of all time, and in some ways the most controversial. Not that there was any doubt about who won," Pep writes in his memoir *Willie Pep Remembers… Friday's Heroes.* "[It was a brawl] like the old-time bare-knuckle days, with wrestling, heeling, tripping, thumbing…. A lot of writers thought that we should have both been thrown out."

Heinz writes that Pep's second fight against Saddler — which he won by decision in 1949, at Madison Square Garden — was "the greatest boxing exhibition I ever saw, for Saddler knocked him out in their first fight, and had the height and reach and punch on him. He hurt him the second time, too, and rocked him time and again, but it was Willie's fight from the first round on when he jabbed Saddler thirty-seven times in succession without a return."

Their historic battles are regarded by many fans and boxing experts as "dirty," but in Pep's excellent book, co-written with Robert Sacchi, he said Saddler wasn't a dirty fighter. Rough, yes, but not dirty!

After Pep and Saddler retired, they became friends. "I have nothing but respect for Sandy," Pep writes.

In the chapter titled "The Trial Horse," one of those Friday night warriors was Ralph "Tiger" Jones who, along with Kid Gavilan and Gaspar Ortega, appeared on national TV during the nineteen-fifties more often than any other fighters.

And when Jones lost it was usually by a split decision!

He was one of the best fighters during the fifties' decade, a decade television viewers, Pep says, "had the chance of seeing about two hundred main events each year on television, and just about every ranking fighter in America. You name the day, they had a fight—Monday night fights, Tuesday night, Wednesday, Thursday, and, of course, the most popular, the Friday Night Fights."

Jones's biggest win was in 1955. In a nationally televised bout from the Chicago Stadium, he defeated Sugar Ray Robinson, who was on the comeback trail. A six-to one underdog, Pep writes, "Tiger gave Ray the worst beating of his career."

Was there a rematch? Robinson's people knew better. According to Pep, their fighter "just couldn't beat [Jones]."

Jones retired in 1962, after fighting professionally for twelve years. He believed, and rightly, that "better management could have given him better purses." Also, if his aggressiveness and ring savvy had been more appreciated by the officials who judged his fights, he would've been awarded more victories and therefore a shot at the middleweight title.

ANOTHER DAY AT THE OFFICE

Kirk Douglas's breakout movie was *Champion*, and after columnist Hedda Hopper saw it, she told him, "You have become a real son of a bitch." The actor responded, saying, "I always was a son of a bitch. You just never noticed."

Released two years after *Champion*, *Detective Story* (1951) is a character study of Douglas's police detective Jim McCleod. It's the kind of role Douglas plays best: Nasty and edgy, a man with a vendetta against everyone. In other words, McCleod is a son of a bitch.

McCleod trusts no one because early in his career he arrested two teenage punks. Taking a chance, he trusted them and had them released. A few days later one of the punks robbed a store and killed the owner. The experience confirmed his belief no one should be trusted.

In a scene with another detective, we learn McCleod first soured on people in his early childhood. "Evil's got a smell of its own," he says to the detective. "A child can spot it. I know, Joe. I know…. I lived with it. I learned it early and deep. My own father was one of those. Every day of my childhood I saw that father of mine with that criminal mind of his abuse and torment my mother and drive her straight to a lunatic asylum. Died there."

Later, in a conversation with William Bendix's detective Lou Brody, McCleod reveals more about himself:

McCleod: All my life I've lived according to principle. I couldn't change even if I wanted to.

Brody: Jim, you gotta bend with the wind or break.

McCleod: Don't be such a mutt. How?

Brody: How? Compromise.

McCleod: How do you compromise? I ain't soft. My mother was soft and it killed her. I don't believe in turning the other cheek.

Douglas's portrayal as a bitter man is exactly right. Perhaps his best screen performance.

In *The Ragman's Son* (1988), the actor's compelling autobiography, he writes of an incident on the set of *Detective Story* involving himself, Joseph Wiseman, whom he described as a "very excitable New York actor," and director William Wyler.

The scene takes place in the police station and calls for Wiseman's psychotic Gennini to shoot McCleod at close range. Though the gun was loaded with blanks, Douglas objected. "I had them put a piece of cheesecloth at twice the distance Joe would be when he shot me," Douglas writes. "I had them fire the blank gun. A couple of hundred holes were in the cheesecloth. I said to Willy, 'How would my face look if that hit me?'"

Wyler re-blocked the scene and Gennini shot McCleod from across the room as the detective advanced toward him. "It was very effective and nobody got hurt," Douglas writes. "This incident added to my reputation as a difficult actor. I didn't care. It added to my life."

HONEST!
HARRY GREB WASN'T HARRY BERG

Berg/Greb

He's positive Harry Greb, the great prizefighter of the Tunney-Dempsey years, was born Harry Berg. He's certain there was enormous prejudice against Jews at the time, and Berg changed his name to Greb because it was easier for a boxer with a non-Jewish name to make a living in the prize ring.

He's wrong about Harry Berg changing his last name to Greb, but on the mark about anti-Semitism.

Harry Greb was born in Pittsburg, PA, in 1894, and died in 1926; Harry Berg was born in New Haven, Connecticut, in 1926, and died in 1994. Harry Greb became one of the best and most feared pugilists of the time; Harry Berg became a policeman and patrolled the Elm City's streets for many years before becoming a well-respected police detective. About four years after he retired, Harry died of lung cancer. Secondhand smoke got him.

Harry Berg's parents were Stuart and Molly Berg and they lived on Campbell Avenue in West Haven for several years before moving to Norton Street in New Haven, where their son was born.

Stocky and short (five feet five), with protruding front teeth, thin brown hair, the Berg/Greb believer had an interesting background, though not a varied one: He was a teacher, then a grammar school principal, and finally a public school superintendent for three years before retiring to a life of mindless leisure.

Dempsey Wanted Nothing to Do with Greb

Nicknamed the Pittsburgh Windmill, Harry Greb fought the great Gene Tunney five times, winning once, drawing once, and losing three times. According to Box-rec.com, he fought thirteen years, compiling a record of 107-8-3, with 48 knockouts. (Some sources claim he had 298 fights.) He fought the best pugilists of his time and was middleweight champion from 1922 to 1923 and light heavyweight champion from 1923 to 1926. He also battled heavyweights, and many boxing historians believe heavyweight champion Jack Dempsey ducked him.

The next time I met the Berg/Greb believer was on a hot Saturday in May, in 2007, and I didn't argue with him about Harry Berg being or not being Harry Greb. Instead, I suggested if he was certain the two Harrys were the same person, he should do some research on Greb, then write an essay titled "Honest! Harry Greg Was Harry Berg." I suggested that he submit it to the *International Boxing Research Organization Journal*, or to another reputable boxing publication.

I paused for effect, then said: "I hope you know you'll be edited, if it's accepted, and you'll have to accept that. Damn it! If you're onto something, go for it! Just think: You'll even have a chance to learn what other boxing fans and historians think!"

No response.

"But you're wrong about Berg being Greb."

No response.

We parted. I knew he wouldn't do any research on his see-how-smart-I-am notion Harry Greb and Harry Berg were the same person.

The Greb Book

I should've handed him a book titled *Smokestack Lightning*, a biography of Harry Greb. Award-winning boxing scholar Springs Toledo, the author of numerous books about the sweet science, is its author.

I should've told the Berg/Greb believer to read page 12, where Toledo writes: "Born June 6, 1894 to a stone mason of severe character from Germany and a mother with roots in Prussia and Bavaria, Greb grew up in a household where schnitzel and sauerkraut were staples, where hard work and good manners were expected and Deutsch was spoken.

"He was baptized 'Eduard Henry' on June 10, at St. Joseph's Church, a German-Catholic parish in the Bloomfield neighborhood of Pittsburgh where he attended school and received the sacraments. Only later did he adopt the name 'Harry' after a baby brother who died in the crib."

I didn't give the Berg/Greb believer the book because he'll believe what he wants to believe, even if the facts say he's wrong. (Yeah, he's one of those types.)

And he has this idea if you admit making a mistake, then you're weak. Bullshit! Perfect example of a lack of self-confidence. But most of the time his personal hygiene is good, and that's a plus.

Come back, Shane!

DOCTOR IN THE VILLAGE

The magic ingredient is that all the characters are absolutely believable... you feel these are real people.... Their lives might be slightly heightened in Portwenn in certain ways, but they are genuine people.

~*Mark Crowdy*
producer, **Doc Martin**

*D*oc Martin, the long running British television series, stars Martin Clunes as Doctor Martin Ellingham. An exceptionally fine physician who cares about his patients, he's often seen running along the twisting streets of the fictional harbor village of Portwenn* attending to the villagers' wide-ranging needs, real or imaginary, and on several occasions saving their lives.

Among his flaws are a pathological dislike of dogs and a phobia causing him to faint and/or vomit at the sight of blood. (That's why he left his practice in London.) Also, because of a loveless upbringing by his parents, it's difficult for him to show affection. (Just ask his wife Louisa, played by the superb Caroline Catz.)

Morwenna Newcross (Jessica Ransom) is Martin's receptionist. She's exceptionally good at her job, and is able to deal with local patients, most of whom are — and this is putting it mildly — idiosyncratic. Also, she's able to withstand Martin's rudeness, condescension, and ill-temper directed at her and anyone else he encounters.

In "Faith,"** one of the series' most memorable episodes, we meet Morwenna's missionary parents, and Martin learns Mrs. Newcross has liver cancer and believes she's dying.

"There's nothing to be done," she says. "And I don't know how to tell my daughter."

"Straight and to the point is usually best," is Martin's response. "Who told you there was nothing to be done? Treatments are advancing all the time."

"My husband and I believe that everything happens for a reason," she says.

"Nonsense," Martin responds.

She thanks him for giving Morwenna a job and for his concern. She has made her peace, she says, and that's her final decision.

When Morwenna has lunch with her parents that afternoon, she learns of her mother's illness. Stunned, she says, "That's why you came back, to tell me that you're dying."

Her father pleads with her to "talk about this as a family." Exasperated, Morwenna says, "Family? Since when did you ever include me? Three months.... You never called or—I've got to go."

At work the next day, she confronts Martin:

Morwenna: Why didn't you tell me about my mum?

Martin: You know I can't discuss my patients with you. She said she was going to tell you.

Morwenna: Yes, but I've been awake half the night thinking about it. (Pause) It's me! I work here. I'm not just some random person off the streets.

Martin: Morwenna, you're upset.

Morwenna: Of course I'm upset. My mum's dying and she's refusing any treatment. I mean, she believes it's just the way things are and that isn't smart.

Martin: No, it isn't. She's being incredibly foolish.

Morwenna: Yes, so convince her. Tell her she's in delayed shock. It's only been three months since diagnosis.

Martin: Three months?

Morwenna: Yeah.

Martin: I'll need to see the scans and test results from the doctor who diagnosed her.

Morwenna: She didn't tell me who the doctor is. She thinks it's part of some great plan. (Pause) Why? Is there something you can do?

Yes, there's something Martin can do and he does it. And that's when we see a different Martin. A Martin who's kind, not brusque. We see Martin at his best!

After contacting Mrs. Newcross's doctor, whose practice is located in Nairobi, Martin diagnoses her condition as hydatid, which, though a serious disease, is treatable.

"It's caused by a parasite found in Africa," he tells the Newcrosses the next day. "It causes tapeworm cysts within the liver. It could easily be mistaken for cancer."

"That means I'm not going to die?" responds Mrs. Newcross.

"Not from this."

Overjoyed, Mr. Newcross claims it's a miracle, but Martin says, "It's not a miracle. It's a parasite."

"No, no. If we hadn't come back here, seen you, she would've died of the hydatid thing, wouldn't she?"

She would've have died, Martin says, if her condition hadn't been diagnosed, to which Mr. Newcross replies, "Well, that's a miracle in my book."

In a television interview, Ransom said Morwenna worked for the neck-brace-wearing Mrs. Sally Tishell (Selina

Cadell), Portwenn's only pharmacist, but was fired because "we didn't get along very well." (Is there anyone in the village who's able to get along with Mrs. Tishell, who by the way has a big-time crush on Doc Martin?)

Prior to that job, she worked in the village bakery, but that didn't last long, either.

"So [Morwenna] wasn't very successful," a BAFTA award winner, explained. By chance she became Doc Martin's receptionist, has "been there for a while," and "can just about put up with his grumpiness. Really, Morwenna tolerates it. She thinks, 'Oh well, he's all right,' and keeps him in his place. It's the job she's had the longest."

My only criticism of the show is that the vibrant Ransom, who has run the London Marathon four times, doesn't get enough screen time.

In real life Portwenn is Port Isaac, a small fishing village located in Cornwall, England, United Kingdom.

**Series 8, episode 4

NOT WHAT HE USED TO BE*

n his book *Murderers' Row*, boxing historian Springs Toledo quotes former middleweight champion Jake LaMotta, who, waxing streetwise and eloquent at the same time, and aware of the many challenges the feared Murderers' Row faced, says: "When those bombers got the chance against a white kid on the square, they sure tried their best to show what they could do, because they all had a dream that maybe they'd get enough of an audience clamoring for them so that someday some promoter would give them the chance they deserved and they'd get a shot at the real money."

Toledo's book—which is also a vivid, exciting history lesson of the era—is impressively researched and focuses on eight members of the Murderers' Row—Cocoa Kid, Lloyd Marshall, Charley Burley, Jack Chase, Aaron Wade, Bert Lytell, Eddie Booker, and Holman Williams—all of whom, the author believes, might've been world champions if they hadn't been ducked by the titleholders of the time.

Champions like Sugar Ray Robinson, whom Burley said he would fight for nothing, and the great Henry Armstrong avoided them. Many leading contenders did too, and, as LaMotta says, promoters treated them shamefully.

Unable to get big money fights, the Murderers' Row warriors often fought each other: Aaron Wade, for instance, battled Williams twice, Burley three times, and Chase three times.

Take the chapter titled "Battle Hymn," which is about Wade (1916-85). Fighting as an amateur, a lightweight, in 1933 he belonged to the Peoria Elks Boxing Team, along with his brother Bruce, a middleweight. "Bruce was good," Toledo writes, "but Aaron was special. Short and wiry with arms so long he looked like he could tie his shoes standing up...." He later "became Peoria's first black Golden Gloves champion."

Nicknamed "Little Tiger," Wade turned professional in 1935 and retired in 1950. In 1943 he fought Archie Moore, at the time the fifth ranked middleweight on the planet, at the Coliseum Bowl in San Francisco.

In his book Toledo gives considerable page time, well-deserved, to Moore, who was six inches taller than the five-foot five Wade and entered the ring a 2-1 favorite. At the end of the fight, Wade's aggressiveness and sharp punching earned him a unanimous decision over the future light heavyweight champion. Wade's most impressive win to date!

Here's the kicker: The September 1944 edition of *Ring* magazine, the so-called bible of boxing, dropped Moore to eighth in the middleweight division while Wade, despite defeating Moore, Toledo writes, "was nowhere to be found in the top ten."

A few years after defeating Moore, Toledo writes, Wade "dissipated. Any substance-abuse counselor will tell you that the bottle is upturned during downtimes and Wade took himself to the Bowery, which was New York City's skid row at the time."

But hold on! There's good news about Wade's life after he retired from the ring. Flash forward to the early 1970s, where he'd be found on McAllister Street, in San Francisco's Fillmore district, at a storefront church: "[He] was now the Reverend Aaron Wade and instead of knocking guys over in the ring he was lifting them up out of the gutter."

"'I'm not what I'm supposed to be as a Christian,' Wade is quoted as saying, 'and not what I'd like to be, but thank God I'm not what I used to be.'"

*"Not What He Used to Be" first appeared in the December 2018/Issue 140 edition of the *International Boxing Research Journal.*

BIRDS SINGING

"He'd make a great interview," said Marv, a fellow reporter and my close friend. Probably the tallest and physically the best conditioned reporter on the staff, Marv was referring to his grandfather, Abraham Greenberg, who spent time during WWII in France.

"One of his stories — I never forgot it — was about the afternoon his company set off for a small village," Marv said. "As they marched they sang about home. My grandfather can fill in details for you about the song and exactly where they were in France. Well, they came across some American soldiers digging a trench. A long trench. My grandfather immediately knew it was a grave for him and the men of his company if they were killed. When his men realized what the trench was for, they stopped singing. My grandfather told me the only sound was a bird singing."

Marv, who sported a raggedy beard and always had tired eyes, stopped talking for a few seconds. Then he continued: "This was one of my grandfather's many war experiences, and he's told it to the family many times. It never changes. He's always been a reader. Loves foreign novelists, especially the Brits and apparently has met a few. Loves to meet writers. Even journalists." Marv grinned, then said: "A self-educated guy. Great imagination. Great storyteller. You'd like him."

"Well, maybe we can hook up next week," I said. "An interview. Not too many of those WWII veterans are with us anymore, you know."

Call it one of life's unexplainable coincidences, but two months ago I finished reading Sebastian Faulks's 1993 novel *Birdsong*, and what Marv told me his grandfather told him and his family about the grave knocked me for a loop.

That night, I took Faulks's WWI novel from my decrepit bookcase, flipped through it until I came to what I was looking for, which was one of the book's most memorable images. A shocker. I read the passage out loud. If you've read the novel, you might remember it: "…the men were obliged to take a farm track across the field…. They sang marching songs with banal, repeated words of home…. As they rounded a corner, [Stephen] saw two dozen men, naked to the waist, digging a hole thirty yards square at the side of the path. For a moment he was baffled. It seemed to have no agricultural purpose…. Then he realized what it was. They were digging a mass grave. He thought of shouting an order to the men to turn about… but they were almost on it, and some of them had already seen their burial place. The songs died on their lips and the air was reclaimed by the birds."

Who was lying? Marv? He befriended me four years ago. A good friend. He helped me out when I first joined the staff. His grandfather Abraham? An old man who—well, maybe his memory is muddled. Or maybe—just maybe—in his travels Abraham met Faulks and told the writer about the soldiers digging a grave for his company, and Faulks used it in his book, because writers use what they need. I mean, they're always on the lookout for material.

I plan to meet Marv's grandfather late next week.

PROPS

One

Props to prizefighters Larry Holmes, Gerry Cooney, and Tommy Hearns.

Two

For sports journalist Jerry Izenberg, in his book *Once There Were Giants: The Golden Age of Heavyweight Boxing*, heavyweight boxing's heyday began on September 25, 1962. That was when Charles "Sonny" Liston knocked out title-holder Floyd Patterson in one round to become world heavyweight champion.

It ended, Izenberg believes, in the mid-nineteen nineties.

Heavyweights Larry Holmes and Gerry Cooney were active during that special time for boxing fans. Several years after his loss to heavyweight champion Holmes on June 11, 1982, Cooney talked with Izenberg about what he called the whole White Hope business—which he hated.

Promoter Don King and Cooney's co-managers Dennis Rappaport and Mike Jones, Izenberg explains, "shamelessly stoked America's subliminal fires of racial fear, pseudo-racial pride, and a large dose of racial hatred. Together, they reached back more than seventy years to recreate what had always been an odious legacy in sports: the 1910 saga of the Great White Hope." That was when Jack Johnson, the first black heavyweight champion, defeated former champion James J. Jeffries, billed as America's Great White Hope. It was a "fight [that wasn't] about Johnson's title [but] all about the color of his skin." Johnson won and "the victory triggered race riots in several cities."

Cooney didn't trust Rappaport and Jones. "'I wanted to be the best fighter I could possibly be, but they gave me guys with great records who were over the hill,'" he told Izenberg. "'I was betrayed by them. I never got the chance to keep learning. They didn't care about me.... They just wanted the immediate payday.'"

From 1980 to 1981 Cooney knocked out heavyweights Jimmy Young, Ron Lyle, and Ken Norton, all past their prime, and Rappaport began proclaiming, "'There will be America, apple pie, Wheaties and Jerry Cooney'" — which proves, Izenberg writes, they "were the wacko twins" and "headline at-any-cost-personalities."

Two nights before Holmes's heavyweight title fight with Cooney, Izenberg dined with the champion and his people. "'Look around this room,' Holmes is quoted as saying. 'Eddie Futch, my trainer, is black. Ray Arcel, my other trainer, is white. Luis Rodriguez, my friend over there, is

Hispanic. My sister-in-law and my secretary at the end of the table are both white.'"

Holmes continued: "'When I say Gerry Cooney is [fighting me for my title] because he's white, I am talking economics. That don't make me a racist. And what he says don't make him a racist either.'"

On fight night Holmes had a character moment. Izenberg writes: After referee Mills Lane gave the fighters their instructions, "Holmes looked Cooney squarely in the eyes and said, just loud enough to be heard by the other fighter above the roar of the Las Vegas record crowd of almost thirty thousand people, 'Let's have a good fight.'"

Cooney's character moment came several days after the fight: He told Izenberg what Holmes said to him before the fight "'was the defining moment for me. The whole burden of all that white bullshit was gone. We were just two fighters about to do what two fighters always do.'"

Three

Unlike Izenberg, sports journalist George Kimball, in his book *Four Kings: The Last Great Era of Boxing*, believes the foursome of Sugar Ray Leonard, Marvelous Marvin Hagler, Roberto Duran, and Tommy Hearns represented boxing's last Golden Age. Their peak years were in the 1980s, and during their careers they fought each other at least once, sometimes twice, and were champions in several weight divisions.

A big moment, one that has stayed with me since it happened in 1986, involved Hearns. (I read about it in a boxing magazine before I read Kimball's book.)

The venue was Caesars Palace in Las Vegas. Aptly nicknamed "Hitman," Hearns, who went on to win world titles in four divisions, was scheduled to fight highly regarded James Shuler of Philadelphia.

Hearns entered the ring with a record of 41-2 (34 KOs). Shuler's record was spotless: Twenty-two wins in as many fights, sixteen of them by knockout. At stake was the North American Boxing Federation middleweight championship.

The fight didn't last long: Boxing beautifully, his left jab repeatedly finding Shuler's face, Hearns set up his opponent with a right cross that knocked him out in the first round. Time: 1:47.

"...a week after [Shuler's] first loss," Kimball writes, "he was dead at twenty-six, killed in a motorcycle accident. Tommy Hearns not only flew to Philadelphia for the funeral, but also returned the NABF belt he had won from Shuler so that his fallen foe would be buried with it."

YOUR LEFT FROM YOUR RIGHT

Author's Note: This incident was told to me by a friend who doesn't want his name revealed. Also, at my friend's request, the name of the newspaper and the people mentioned in the essay have been changed.

've been a reporter for the *Getsville Courier* for eight years.

On May 12, 2005, I telephone Mr. Ennis Mulbloom, the celebrated author of numerous self-help books. I introduce myself and explain I'd like to schedule an interview with him. He says tomorrow, mid-morning, would be an appropriate time to meet. He gives me directions to his residence, accompanied by an enigmatic warning that the path to his home is, as he put it, "fraught with danger."

He pauses. Then: "Park on Lowman Road. Take the first path on your right—you can't miss it. You'll soon come to a wooden bridge. Cross it and take the first right onto another path, which is narrow. After a few yards you'll encounter a ditch located on your right. A word of caution: The ditch, which isn't deep, seems to have a life of its own. Keep walking. You'll soon reach my domicile."

I thank him. He thanks me.

At ten-thirty the next morning I park my car on Lowman Road. I follow Ennis Mulbloom's directions.

After I cross the bridge, I see the ditch. It looks as if it's calmly waiting for someone to topple into it. I'm tempted to make an obscene gesture in its direction. Instead, I gingerly sidestep it. I spontaneously mumble a quick thank you to St. Anthony, though I'm not Catholic. (A friend once told me St. Anthony is the patron saint of unexpected tumbles.)

I continue walking. A few minutes later I arrive at Ennis Mulbloom's ramshackle house.

I knock on his door. Ennis Mulbloom opens it. Tall and bearded, all business, he greets me sternly. I follow him into his kitchen. He motions me to sit down at the large oak table, which seems out of place in such a small kitchen.

I begin asking questions about his latest book. I take copious notes as he speaks. He answers my questions without changing his dour expression, but he comes to life when he responds to my last question about life in the twenty-first century. With total certainty he says how much smarter our conservative generation—we're both in our late-sixties—is than today's young adults, college grads or otherwise.

I nod in agreement.

He tightened up as he spoke. Said something about these young people not knowing their left from their right....

I keep nodding.

When the interview is finished, we shake hands. I promise to send him the piece when it's published.

Outside I notice how chilly it has become. I begin walking with haste. Before I cross the bridge, I look to my right for the ditch. It isn't there. Somewhat puzzled, I step backward across the path several steps — and feel myself falling.

More embarrassed than hurt, I climb out of the ditch. Once on my feet, I brush myself off and try to regain my composure. I hope no one has witnessed my misstep.

I return home without further incident.

Later that evening I pour myself a whiskey, sit at my desk, open my laptop and begin writing the interview.

I wonder if I should include Ennis Mulbloom's remarks about how much smarter our generation is than today's current crop of left-leaning young adults.

FEAR THE HOUSE OF SILK

1. A Yarder Named Lestrade

*T*he *House of Silk* by Anthony Horowitz, the award-winning writer of the dramatic British series *Foyle's War*, is a novel about Sherlock Holmes, with adequate page time devoted to Holmes's rival, Inspector Lestrade of Scotland Yard.

As expected, Holmes doesn't have a high opinion of the Inspector. For example, when Carstairs, one of Holmes's clients, says that Lestrade "'struck me as being both thorough and efficient,'" the master detective counters, "'I can assure you that if Lestrade is involved [in any case], you can be quite certain that he will come to a conclusion very quickly, even if it is completely wrong.'"

Conversely, Dr. John Watson, Holmes's assistant, friend, and biographer, praises Lestrade as "a capable man and someone who goes to a crime scene in search of evidence, as opposed to Holmes's method in solving a crime, which is with his intellect, in his comfortable living quarters."

(Watson adds that Holmes once grudgingly admitted that Inspector Lestrade is persistent.)

2. His One Friend

Holmes is patronizing, intimidating, and moody. He has no doubt he's superior to everyone he meets, including his best friend Watson, who's probably his only friend.

Anyway, who'd want to be friends with Sherlock Holmes?

3. Dead Body

Early on in the novel there's a revealing scene between Holmes and Lestrade that takes place at Mrs. Oldmore's Private Hotel, where a dead body has been discovered and identified as the infamous Keelan O'Donaghue, an American criminal in England on a mission of revenge.

After examining the corpse and listening to Holmes's theories about what happened, Lestrade loses his patience and proclaims: "'The trouble with you, Holmes, is that you have a way of complicating things. I sometimes wonder if you don't do it deliberately. It's as if you need the crime to rise to the challenge, as if it has to be unusual enough for it to be worth solving and it is easy to construe what took place here.... The two of them fell out. The other pulled a knife. This is the result!'"

Before he leaves the apartment, Lestrade sarcastically tells Holmes, "'I'm sure we'll run into each other again, Mr. Holmes. And if you need me, you know where to find me.'"

"'If I should ever find myself in need of Inspector Lestrade, things will have come to a pretty pass,'" Holmes says to Watson after Lestrade has left.

4. Hurtful

Though Lestrade likes Watson, given the chance he relishes being hurtful to Holmes. Take the scene when the savagely mutilated body of a thirteen-year-old boy is discovered.

To Holmes, Lestrade says with delight: "'I hoped you might be able to shed some light on the matter. It may be, after all, that this is your fault.... I warned you about mixing with these children. You employed the boy. You set him on the trail of a known criminal. I grant you, he may have had his own ideas and they may have been the ruin of him. But this is the result.'"

Stung by Lestrade's words, Holmes realizes he bears some responsibility for the youngster's death: On their way back to Baker Street, Watson tells us, "Holmes sunk back into the corner of the hansom and for much of the way he sat in silence, refusing to meet my eyes."

5. The Irregulars

Ross was the murdered youngster's name and one of Holmes's Baker Street Irregulars. Threadbare, homeless, roaming the London streets, their ages between eight and fifteen, the Irregulars made their debut in Arthur Conan Doyle's 1887 novel *A Study in Scarlet*.

Occasionally Holmes hired them for assistance in his crime solving efforts. "'There's more work to be got out of one of those little beggars than out of a dozen of the force,'" he tells Watson. "'The mere sight of an official-looking person seals men's lips. These youngsters, however, go everywhere and hear everything. They are as sharp as needles, too; all they want is organization.'"

6. Mrs. Hudson and Mycroft

Horowitz's intriguing novel is filled with memorable and important minor characters. Along with Lestrade, there are Mrs. Hudson and Mycroft Holmes.

Mrs. Hudson is the housekeeper and landlady of 221B Baker Street, where Holmes resides. "It is somehow comforting to me, all these years later," Watson says, "to reflect that she knew him better than anyone and had put up with all manner of peculiarities during the lengthy period that he was with her."

(Peculiarities? His violin playing at all hours of the day and night, his cocaine addiction, his mood swings, and his clients, who are often, Watson says, "desperate and undesirable.")

Mrs. Hudson, who rarely complained about Holmes, remained "loyal to the end," says Dr. Watson, and though she "flits in and out of my pages, I actually knew very little about her, not even how she came to occupy the property at 22IB Baker Street.... [I wished I] had conversed with her more and taken her for granted a little less."

~~~

In his book about Winston S. Churchill, *Darkest Hour*, Anthony McCarten speculates on a meeting between Churchill and Lord Halifax. I'll do the same now concerning an exchange between Holmes and Watson regarding Holmes's brother Mycroft. What Holmes said shocked Watson:

Holmes: Yes, Watson. Mycroft is absolutely brilliant.

Watson: I wonder had he become a detective, would he have been able to handle the job.

Holmes: (Pause) If he decided to become a detective, he would have been my equal.

Watson: Goodness.

Holmes: Or even my superior.

Mycroft has a flaw, however. A telling one. As Watson puts it, "Mycroft Holmes suffered from... a streak of indolence so ingrained that it would have rendered him unable to solve any crime, for the simple reason he would have been unable to interest himself in it."

As for the House of Silk, Mycroft warns Holmes and Watson not to become involved with it, that "'it was indeed the subject of a police investigation,'" and that the murder of young Ross, "'as tragic as it may be is completely insignificant when set against the wider picture.'"

7. Holmes's Recovery

Because Watson's wife is away in London visiting friends, he stays with Holmes at the detective's Baker Street lodging. His intention is to keep an eye on Holmes because "when he was idle [and] his energies were not being directed towards some insoluble mystery, he became distracted and prone to long moods of depression. But this time, I realized, it was something more."

Watson knows what Holmes had discovered about the House of Silk and the horrors that transpired inside it "had left an indelible mark on his consciousness. Nobody knew evil like Holmes, but there are some evils that it is better not to know...."

To recover his sanity Holmes knows he must destroy the House of Silk. One evening, soon after the House of Silk mystery has been solved, he informs Watson he's going out.

"'What I need is a little time alone,'" he says.

Horowitz doesn't tell us what Holmes did that night. Instead, Watson makes the discovery the next morning. Holmes's coat, Watson tells us, "which had been hanging in its usual place, had the strong smell of cinders."

Though Holmes has been emotionally damaged after the House of Silk nightmare, rest assured he's returning to normal: As Watson puts it, "That evening, Holmes played his Stradivarius for the first time in a while. I listened with pleasure to the soaring tune as we sat together on either side of the hearth."

DREAM A DREAM

Author's Note: "Dream a Dream" was inspired by a dream I had several years ago. Now it's an essay (with questions) that I hope reads and feels like a short story.

I'm walking along a muddy path surrounded by trees, their branches leafless and reaching out for attention. I stop walking because I feel something attach itself above my left ankle. It's gray. Slug-like. It makes a slurping sound. I bend over and tear it from my leg, hold it tightly in my hand, and watch it curl up. It spits yellow liquid at me.

I throw it into the woods to my right.

Then I wake up. Pee time. Three o'clock. So, I stagger into the bathroom. I pee, return to bed, fall asleep quickly, and begin dreaming again. But this dream is different from the first one. It's about parking my car in an indoor parking lot in New Haven and walking several blocks to a large building, entering…

…and when I leave the building I realize I've forgotten where I parked my car.

Snap! Just like that I'm back in my first dream walking on the same path. I look at my ankle. There's no damage. I continue walking, though slower than before, because I look more often at the ground for another slug-like creature, while praying someone will come to my aid and take me out of the woods, to my home.

But I know that if someone enters my dream, he's dreaming too, and do I really want someone from another dream invading my dream?

Soon, rearing up in front of me and blocking my way is a creature of immense size. It moves near me and with one of its claws picks me up and brings me close to its mouth. I smell its foul breadth and see its double-edged teeth. It's drooling and readying to grind me into small bits.

I wake up.

I'm back to complete reality… in my own bed… sweating but awake, knowing I'll soon be facing….

And now, reader, your job is to pick the best answer from the five choices below. Be ready to defend your selection verbally.

a) **a bright, calm day….**

b) the realization that it was all a nightmare and I had nothing to worry about....

c) a cold shower, a decent breakfast, and an exciting day at work....

d) the nightmare of the waking world from which there would be no waking....

e) another uneventful day and a chance to stop at Gronsky's Pub for a potation after work....

Your answer: _____

Why?_____

_____

_____

_____

_____

_____

_____

TAKE ANOTHER BOW, MR. HEFLIN

In 1949, several years before Van Heflin's appearance in Arthur Miller's drama, *A View from the Bridge*, he co-starred with Robert Ryan in director Fred Zinnemann's *Act of Violence*, a masterful *film noir* highly praised by critics and moviegoers.

The film begins at night, somewhere in New York, and we see tall, trench-coated, limping Joe Parkson (Ryan). Armed with a .45 pistol, he boards a bus for a small town in California.

His mission: To kill Heflin's Frank Enley, a war hero and one of the town's most prominent, well-respected citizens.

For the first half of the movie, Enley is the character with whom we sympathize. On the other hand, Parkson is a disturbed, dangerous man. In the second half we learn why he's stalking Enley. Why he wants him dead.

Since the war ended, Enley has been hiding a horrific secret—and Parkson knows what it is. Hoping to escape from Parkson, he flees to the Blake Hotel in Los Angeles, where a convention is taking place. Followed there by his wife Edith (Janet Leigh), he tells her why Parkson is pursuing him.

Enley: After we were shot down and sent to a prison camp—Joe, myself, some other officers. I was the senior officer responsible for the rest of the men. Toward the end it got—we were all starving to death. Went crazy. One day Joe came to me. They dug a tunnel, he and some of the others, and were going to try to escape. I told him not to do it. I begged him not to do it.

The week before in the British section twelve men had been shot for the same thing. Told him they didn't stand a chance. They'd be dead before they started. He wouldn't listen to me. I lay awake all night trying to think of some way of stopping him. The next morning, I went to the prison commandant. I made a deal with him. I said that I'd tell him if he'd go easy on the men. He promised. Word of an officer.

So, I waited. Waited all day. I thought the guards would close up the tunnel, do something, but they didn't.... That night I tried to talk to Joe again, but he wouldn't pay any attention.... Well, they started through, and then I heard the guards at the other end of the tunnel. They set a trap for them. They bayonetted them. They set dogs on 'em, and when it was over they didn't even shoot them. They just left them there.

Acting with his voice, body and eyes, Heflin's powerful emoting takes us inside Enley's soul, and we understand the guilt and torment with which he has been living for many years.

Another notable scene occurs late in the movie and involves Parkson and his girlfriend Ann (an excellent Phyllis Thaxter). In their room at the Blake Hotel, she tries reasoning with him. "Are you the law?" she asks. "What makes you think you're so much better than [Enley] is? Whatever he's done he tried to make up for it. He's lived a decent, useful life. But what have you done? What are you going to prove anyway with your vengeance, your violence? You aren't going to bring those men back. You're just going to smash a few more lives, his wife, his son, me."

Her words don't change Parkson's mind. Becoming desperate, her voice loud, Ann says, "Even if you go through with this, no matter if they kill you or put you in jail, even if they say you're sick and half-crazy and let you off easy, you're finished, Joe. You're washed up. You're as crippled in your mind as in your—"

She stops talking. Knowing her remark about Parkson being "crippled" is hurtful, she apologizes to him and says that once she made him happy and can do it again.

Her plea doesn't change his mind because he's obsessed with killing Enley.

At the end of the film there's a confrontation between Parkson and Enley which is, Derek Sculthorpe writes in *Van Heflin: A Life in Film*, "both compelling and uplifting. All along, the audience is made to feel for the characters and sympathies switch from Enley to Parkson and with a true appreciation for both."

THE KEY TO THE WHOLE SHEBANG

The film adaptation of Frederick Knott's stage play, Alfred Hitchcock's *Dial M for Murder* (1954), doesn't possess the physical action of *To Catch a Thief* and *North by Northwest*. In those flicks Cary Grant was on the run from start to finish.

In *Dial M Murder*, Ray Milland's impeccably dressed and insufferably smug Tony Wendice plans to murder his wife Margot (Grace Kelly)—he believes it'll be the perfect crime—because she's two-timing him with mystery writer Mark Halliday (Robert Cummings). They aren't aware Tony knows of their affair and plans to hire a man named Swann (the ultra-sinister Anthony Dawson) to kill Margo.

More important: Wendice didn't expect to be matching wits with Inspector Hubbard (the suave John Williams, he of *To Catch a Thief* and here the proud possessor of a perfect mustache.)

Unflappable and almost as smug as Wendice, Williams is either doing a great imitation of George Sanders, or for years Sanders had been doing one of him. (That's right! George Sanders, the actor about whom The Kinks in "Celluloid Heroes" sang, "If you covered him with garbage, George Sanders would still have style.")

By the way, everyone in this movie is smartly groomed, though admittedly Kelly's Margot appears haggard when we see her attired in her prison garb and awaiting trial for Swann's murder. (That's right. While she was being attacked, Margot, ever resourceful, stabbed Swann to death.)

Latchkey, Latchkey Where Art Thou?

Careful! You might have nightmares about latchkeys after you see this flick. I'm serious. Consider this scene near the end of the movie, in the Wendice's apartment:

Halliday: If [Margot's key] was there [under the stair carpet], why didn't Wendice use it just now?

Hubbard: He didn't use it because he doesn't realize it's there. He still thinks it's in his wife's handbag. You see, you were very nearly right. He told Swann that he would leave your latchkey under the stair carpet, Mrs. Wendice, and told him to return it to the same place *when* he left. But as Swann was killed we naturally assumed that your key would be in one of Swann's pockets. That was his little mistake because Swann had done exactly as you suggested, Mr. Halliday. He unlocked the door, then returned the key before he came in.

Halliday: It's been out there ever since... and the key Wendice took out of Swann's pocket and returned to her handbag—

Hubbard:—was Swann's own latchkey. (Pause) Mind you, even I didn't guess that at once. Extraordinary. It always puzzled me that no key was found on Swann's body. After all, most men carry a latchkey about with them. Then I had a brain wave! I took the key that was in your handbag to his girlfriend's, Mrs. Van Dorn's, and unlocked the door of her flat...then I borrowed her telephone and called Scotland Yard.

Mrs. Wendice: Why did you bring me here?

Hubbard: Because you were the only other person who could possibly have left that key outside. I had to find out if you knew it was there.

Mrs. Wendice: Suppose I had known?

Hubbard: (Smiling confidently) You didn't.

Where was the latchkey—who put it there— why was it there—was it still there—did someone take it—Margot's handbag—carrying a latchkey—the stair carpet— Swann's pocket—the key that was in your handbag—Mrs. Van Dorn— Swann's unlocked door—the latchkey is under the stair carpet....

If your head's spinning, join the club!

In the latchkey scene the movie's major characters are assembled in the Wendice's apartment, and the first time you see the scene, you accept it without question. But perhaps two hours later, relaxing at home, sipping on a Genesee

Cream Ale, you'll begin questioning what you saw and realize Hitchcock is having fun with his audience. After all, it's his movie.

AND WHAT A FIGHTER HE WAS!*

The young heavyweight was up against the wily veteran, thought to be past his prime. Coley Wallace was the young fighter's name, his opponent Cleveland's Jimmy Bivins.

They were fighting on September 24, 1962, at St. Nicholas Arena, located in New York, New York. It was one of those iconic Friday Night Fights sponsored by Gillette Blue Blades.

(If you recall the tune, reader, take a moment and sing along: Look sharp! Feel sharp! Be sharp! And listen, mister: How are you fixed for blades? Do you have plenty? How are you fixed for blades? You better check! Please make sure you have enough cuz a worn out blade makes shavin' mighty tough. How are you fixed for blades? Do you have enough? Gillette Blue Blades, I mean.)

When the bell sounded for round nine, Harlem's Wallace was ahead on the officials' score cards. Sixteen pounds lighter and several inches shorter than Wallace, Bivins threw a perfect right hand punch that landed on Wallace's jaw and knocked him cold.

Cold!

A one punch knockout is a thing of beauty! Walcott knocking out Charles.... Marciano knocking out Walcott.... Moore knocking out Davidson.... Robinson knocking out Fullmer. One punch. Curtains! More exciting than a hole in one, a hat trick, a no hitter.

Granted, Bivins wasn't the fighter he had been in the nineteen-forties, when he was one of the world's best light heavyweights and heavyweights, but that night against Wallace he proved he still had some kick.

~~~

Bivins began fighting professionally in 1940 and retired in 1955. He compiled an 85-25-1 (31 KOs/ KO by 5) record. In 1999, he was inducted into the International Boxing Hall of Fame. He died July 4, 2012.

~~~

Boxing historian and scholar Jerry Fitch writes about Bivins in his meticulously researched, excellently written biography *James Louis Bivins: The Man Who Would be Champion*. According to Fitch, "1952 basically summed up the way Jimmy's career went from 1946 on. He wasn't fighting often but still commanded a rating and was listed #10 heavyweight for the period ending May 18, 1952, by *Ring* magazine."

Bivins's best boxing years were from 1942 to 1945, and "what he accomplished during those three years was simply amazing," Fitch writes. His performances in the squared circle during that time "launched him to the top of the ratings [in both] the light heavyweight and heavyweight divisions. If he ever deserved a title shot that truly had to be the time."

On January 7, 1943, Bivins decisioned tough Anton Christoforidis to became duration light heavyweight champion. A month later he won the duration heavyweight title, defeating Tami Mauriello by decision.

(What was a duration champion? While "heavyweight champion Joe Louis and other champions were serving in World War II," Fitch explains, "their titles were frozen." Newspapers and some boxing promoters created temporary champions, "the idea [being] to bridge the gap and create some excitement.")

Written with the enthusiasm and knowledge of his other boxing books, Fitch's superb biography of a fighter who should be better known and appreciated in boxing circles is packed with images of Bivins and many of the fighters he fought.

*"And What A Fighter He Was!" was first published in the December 2017 issue of the *International Boxing Research Journal*.

TO THE RESCUE!

Before Joe Penhale (John Marquez) became Portwenn's Police Constable, in the long-running British series *Doc Martin*, he worked for the London Police. While on duty one day, he was kicked in the head by a horse, which caused his agoraphobia and narcolepsy.

In addition, his wife left him.

This, too: Though Doc Martin (Martin Clunes), the harbor village's physician, considers him incompetent, Penhale always means well. Always. And he's dedicated to his work.

In the episode titled "Departure" (series 6), Penhale steps up—big time. Doc Martin's wife Louisa (Caroline Catz) is struck by a car and hospitalized. After she returns home from the hospital, she decides to leave Martin. Reasons: She's no longer able to tolerate his lack of social skills and his unwillingness—or inability—to show emotion.

(Martin's aunt, Dr. Ruth Ellingham, a retired psychiatrist and one of the few sane inhabitants of Portwenn, tells him, "And you love Louisa. Yet you shut down and shut down and shut down until you pushed her away.")

With her and Martin's infant child James Henry, Louisa travels to the airport and boards a plane.

When Martin learns her injury needs immediate attention—it's more serious than originally believed—he and PC Penhale speed to the airport to prevent her and James Henry from leaving. At the airport Martin approaches a security guard who's clearly impressed with himself and refuses to let Martin board the plane. An argument ensues and Martin becomes angry.

Martin: .... A patient of mine is on a plane and may require urgent medical attention.

Security Guard: No. Haven't heard any reports of that.

Martin: This is a report. Just let me pass.

Security Guard: I have to ask you to step back, sir, before I call the police.

Enter PC Penhale.

"They're already here," Penhale says. "Let this man through. It's an emergency."

The guard asks, "You're a policeman?" and Penhale says, "Yes, I am a policeman. But it's my day off."

Self-righteously, the guard warns Penhale to "move back before I call the real police."

Stepping in front of Martin and looking directly at the guard, Penhale says, "This man's wife needs urgent medical attention. If that plane takes off she could die. Now, do you want that on your conscience, knowing that you could've saved her life, because you are an officious little man who refused to listen?"

Penhale's honest directness works: Martin boards the plane and removes Louisa and James Henry.

Kudos for Joe Penhale: He refuses to be stonewalled by the security guard and proves that a person known for his incompetence can on occasion become competent at what he does.

COSMIC TUMBLERS

Married, with one child, she's seated comfortably in her home library finishing the book she has been assigned to review, Winston Churchill's 1930 memoir *The Early Years: 1879-1904*.

She reviews books for a local newspaper. That's her job.

In an early chapter of his memoir, Churchill wrote about the two nightmare years he spent as a student at St. James, a private school for boys in lower Darwen, England. The young Churchill was usually at the bottom of his class and disliked by his classmates. Flogging was routine and kindness rare.

He hated the place.

The book reviewer decided to concentrate her review on Churchill's early schooling, citing his three most poignant remarks about that terrible time in his life:

First: "Where my reason, imagination or interest were not engaged, I would not or could not learn."

Second: "The greatest pleasure I had was reading." (For young Churchill reading was "a refuge" and his favorite book was Robert Louis Stevenson's *Treasure Island*, which his father gave him when he was nine-and-a-half years old.) "I remember the delight with which I devoured [the book]."

Third: "My teachers saw me at once backward and precocious, reading books beyond my years and yet at the bottom of the Form."

In her review, she elaborated on those remarks.

The book reviewer's love of history and writing was passed on to her daughter, a precocious and lively girl named Candice, who many years later went on to write three critically acclaimed best-sellers: *The River of Doubt* (2005), the award-winning *Destiny of the Republic* (2011), and *The Hero of the Empire*, which focuses on the twenty-five-year old Churchill's escape from a Boer prison in 1899.

On this particular morning the "cosmic tumblers" W.P. Kinsella wrote about in his novel *Shoeless Joe* quietly clicked into place and "what is possible" happened for the book reviewer. Removing herself from her comfortable chair, she walked to her well-stocked bookcase and took from it a book that wouldn't be published for many years, her daughter's critically acclaimed, best-selling *Hero of the Empire*.

When she returned to her chair, the book opened itself to the chapter Candice had devoted to *Kidnapped*, another Stevenson novel that played a key role in Church-ill's life.

After his escape from the Boer prison, Churchill hid in Witbank, a mining town, located east of Pretoria. There the man who risked his life by hiding him, a mine manager named John Howard, gave him a copy of *Kidnapped*.

Churchill discovered what Candice in her book called "a shared understanding" between *Kidnapped*'s main character, seventeen-year-old David Balfour, and himself. Balfour was, Candice writes, "a fictional character, [but] through him Stevenson expressed the same feelings of foreboding, powerlessness, even shame, with which Churchill was struggling...."

She quotes Churchill: "'Those thrilling pages... awakened sensations with which I was only too familiar. To be a fugitive, to be a hunted man, to be wanted, is a mental experience by itself.... The risks of the battlefield, the hazards of the bullet or the shell are one thing. Having the police after you is another. The need for concealment and deception breeds an actual sense of guilt very undermining to morale. Feeling that at any moment the officers of the law may present themselves gnawed the structure of self-confidence.'"

Two days later, after Candice's mother finished editing her review of Churchill's memoir, Kinsella's tumblers struck again: What she had read in her daughter's book was erased from her memory. Completely erased!

That evening the book reviewer read her review for the last time. When she finished reading, she was filled with a mother's pride because she knew someday her daughter would write a book about Winston S. Churchill.

TRAVEL WELL, MARGOT

Margot Kidder's breakthrough role was her portrayal of Lois Lane in *Superman: The Movie* (1978). As Clark Collis writes in *Entertainment Weekly*, "Kidder's no-nonsense portrayal [of Lois] remains, for many, the definitive onscreen version."

The Canadian-born actress, who appeared in 130 big and small screen productions, died on May 13, 2018, at the age of sixty-nine. A suicide.

As a teenager Kidder had severe emotional problems, attempting suicide when she was fourteen. As an adult her acting career was derailed by her struggle with bipolar disorder.

The Week (May 25, 2018) points out that in 1996 she had a nervous breakdown and "was found in a stranger's backyard outside Los Angeles. 'If you're gonna fall apart,' the actress later joked, 'do it in your own bedroom.'"

In *Salon* Gwenda Bond writes that Kidder, always honest about her illness, "went on to struggle publicly with bipolar disorder, and again refused to be shamed for that. Instead she became a powerful voice of honesty about mental health issues… [She] played many parts in her life—actress, mental health advocate, and activist…."

Kidder and Christopher Reeve share the spotlight in Richard Donner's *Superman: The Movie*—and that's what's best about it.

Their most unforgettable moment is her interview with Superman that takes place in the evening on her patio. Watch her reactions when she asks him, *Are you married? Do you have a girlfriend? How old are you? How tall are you? And how much do you weigh? The rest of your bodily functions are, er, normal? Do you eat? Well, then (laughing), is it true that you can see through anything? And that you're totally impervious to pain?*

For me, watching Kidder in movies and television always touched a nerve, and one of her earliest movies, *Sisters* (1972), was director Brian de Palma's first homage to Alfred Hitchcock. Her performance was praised by Leonard Maltin, in *Leonard Maltin's Movie Encyclopedia,* as "an accomplished, eerie interpretation of separated Siamese twins." An overlooked horror gem, it was scored by Bernard Hermann, Hitchcock's favorite composer.

Released five years before *Superman: The Movie*, Jennifer Salt plays Grace Collier, a spunky Staten Island investigative reporter who witnesses a grisly murder from her apartment window. As expected, the police don't believe her. Like Hitchcock's movie *Rear Window* (1954), the classic James Stewart and Grace Kelly starrer, she conducts her own investigation.

TIGER ON THE ICE

D ave "Tiger" Williams's autobiography, *Tiger – A Hockey Story*, co-written with James Lawton, immediately wins the reader's trust thanks to the author's candor, humor, and knowledge of the game he played for seventeen National Hockey League seasons.

Some statistics: Williams played in 962 games, scored 241 goals, and collected 272 assists. His 3,966 penalty minutes are the most ever by a NHL player.

When he played for the Toronto Maple Leafs (1974-80), a fierce rivalry developed between him and Terry O'Reilly of the Boston Bruins. It was in a game during the 1975-76 season, in Toronto, that O'Reilly wrestled him to the ice. Enter Wayne Cashman, who tried kicking Williams in the head with his skates. "He got one in through my helmet," Williams writes. "It was then that O'Reilly said, low enough to escape Cashman's hearing, 'Put your head under my body. I'll shield you.' I guess he believed that Cashman was capable of kicking my eyes out."

From that point on Williams respected O'Reilly. "I would never elbow him, cheap shot him," he writes. When they played against each other, Williams played hard "but clean.... O'Reilly did all he could by warning me and shielding me, and he hoped I wouldn't tell anyone in my dressing room. A guy with a reputation for toughness wouldn't want people to think he was softening, slipping."

Another player Williams respected was Montreal's Larry Robinson, one of the NHL's premier defensemen. In 1979 the Leafs had reached the Stanley Cup quarter-finals and were trailing Montreal three games to none. In the fourth game, in overtime, referee Bob Myers penalized Williams for ostensibly high-sticking Robinson.

"It was a horseshit call and it cost us the game," Williams writes.

Irony! It was Robinson who scored the winning goal and seconds later an incensed Williams jumped out of the penalty box and went after referee Myers. "I wanted to kill the son of a bitch," he writes. "Robinson must have seen something in my eyes, because he headed right for me and grabbed me; only a guy as big, strong and fast as Robinson could have done it. He wrapped his big arms around me and said, 'Forget it, kid... but I'll take you fishing in the summer.' The big guy saved my neck all right, because if I'd got hold of Myers, I'm sure I would have done him serious damage.'"

Another tough guy, Dave "The Hammer" Schultz of the Philadelphia Flyers, piled up 2294 minutes in 535 games in an eleven-year NHL career. Williams writes that Schultz was his team's "big man, but I was never overly impressed with him" because he was "an outright bully."

What Schultz lacked "in the end was mental toughness," Williams writes. "It was the same with a lot of those Philadelphia guys." One of them was Don Saleski. When he played for the Broad Street Bullies, he was a tough guy because he had "the wolf pack" to protect him.

Later when he played with the Colorado Rockies and was "on his own," it was "a different story. We were looking for guys like that when Philadelphia broke up.... I would classify them as guys who like to play tough, do a lot of mouthing off when they have a couple of gorillas at their side."

During Williams's era Edmonton's Dave Semenko served as Wayne Gretzky's bodyguard. "To play Semenko's role, you have to be a rare breed of hockey player," Williams writes. "He gets only sufficient ice time to fulfill his main function, which is to intimidate... he seems happy in his work... he's big and mean... I know he wants to get me, that he really hates me. That's probably because I take every chance I get to run at Gretzky."

Williams describes Gretzky as an "incredible" player, but "everybody knows that Semenko's worth at least 25 goals a season to Gretzky."

THEY'RE ALMOST EACH OTHER

Near the end of Michael Mann's *Heat* (1995), a stylized gangster movie and character study of two men on opposite sides of the law, there's an unforgettable showdown between Al Pacino's obsessive cop Vincent Hanna and Robert De Niro's career criminal Neil McCauley.

A chase. Gunshots. Hanna shoots McCauley whose last words are, "I told you I'd never go back [to jail]." Hanna says, "I know," followed by a close-up, as he and McCauley clasp hands. For McCauley there's oblivion, for Hanna re-morse because he knows the criminal he killed is his mirror image.

Early on, in the film's signature scene, Pacino and De Niro, two of America's best actors, meet for the first time in a restaurant. Haunting, convincing, and quietly frightening is the best way to describe it.

McCauley calmly reminds Hanna that he will not, under any circumstances, even if it means death, go back to prison. As they talk they learn about each other.

McCauley: I do what I do best. I take scores. You do what you do best. Try to stop guys like me.

Hanna: So, you don't want a regular type life?

McCauley: What the fuck is that—barbecues and ballgames?

Hanna: Yeah.

McCauley: This regular-type life—that your life?

Hanna: No. My life's a disaster zone. I got a step-daughter so fucked up because her real father is this large-type asshole. I got a wife. We're passing each other on the downslope of a marriage. My third. Because I spend all my time chasing guys like you around the block. That's my life.

McCauley: Guy told me one time don't let yourself get attached to anything you are not willing to walk out on in thirty seconds flat if you feel the heat around the corner. (Pause) Well, if you're on to me and you got to move when I move, how do you expect to keep a marriage?

Hanna: That's an interesting point. What are you a monk?

McCauley: I have a woman.

Hanna: What do you tell her?

McCauley: I tell her I'm a salesman.

Hanna: So then, if you spot me coming around that corner, you're just going to walk out on this woman. Not say goodbye?

McCauley: That's the discipline.

Hanna: That's pretty vacant.

McCauley says the discipline has to be accepted, that there's no choice, but if it isn't accepted "we both better do something else." Then comes the movie's big revelation: They both agree that they don't want to do anything else.

What's left unsaid, except in their eyes, is that it's their destiny to have a deadly confrontation.

AND SHIRLEY BECAME SHELLEY

One of John Garfield's costars in 1951's *He Ran All the Way* is a young woman from St. Louis, Missouri, named Shirley Schrift, who later became Shelley Winters and went on to win two Academy Awards for Best Supporting Actress.

In *He Ran All the Way*, which John Berry directed, she plays Peg Dobbs, a bakery worker attracted to Garfield's Nick Robey.

On the run from the law for murdering a guard during a warehouse robbery, Robey, while holding Peg, her parents, and younger brother hostage in their New York flat, brings something new and exciting and dangerous into Peg's uneventful life.

Torn emotionally between the paranoid Robey and staying with her family, Peg decides to leave with him. Near the end of the movie, as they are ready to leave, her father intervenes. He and Robey have a gun battle.

Peg makes a decision from which she'll never recover: She grabs Robey's gun and shoots him. In a powerhouse ending, he staggers outside the apartment and dies on the rain-soaked New York City street.

What made Winters's performance so convincing was that she internalized her emotions and didn't have to say how she felt: Viewers knew by watching her and so did her costars.

In one of her early movies, *A Double Life* (1947), Winters played Pat Kroll, a waitress in an Italian restaurant who befriends Shakespearean actor Anthony John (Ronald Colman in an Oscar winning turn), and then is murdered by him.

In her autobiography *Also Known as Shirley*, Winters writes that her first scene with Colman was a disaster: "I stumbled in. I poured coffee on [his] hands. I poured coffee in his lap. I dropped my pad." And yes, there's more: "I poured coffee in the water glass, and it overflowed. I kept four prop men and the wardrobe department cleaning up after me. It wasn't funny; it was a nightmare."

When director George Cukor called for a break, Colman asked Winters to join him for lunch at the commissary. She agreed. They talked, Colman telling her humorous stories to put her at ease. When she returned to the set and did the scene again, she nailed it.

"I have always been eternally grateful to Ronald Colman for the way he made me relax at that lunch," Winters writes. "He made me feel that I was somehow in his league, thus saving my role in the film and perhaps my career. I will always love him for his kindness and perception."

MEET REVEREND HARRY POWELL

Set during the Depression, *The Night of the Hunter* (1955) stars Robert Mitchum as Harry Powell, a self-proclaimed, maniacal, hymn-singing, serial killing preacher who first charms and then marries gullible women for their money.

Then he murders them.

After his cellmate Ben Harper (Peter Graves) is executed, Powell seeks out his wife Willa (Shelley Winters), and marries her. She doesn't know he's after the ten thousand dollars her husband robbed and hid.

Willa is his next victim. The chilling image of her at the bottom of the river, behind the wheel of a car, her hair flowing, is horrific. Impossible to forget.

Her two children, John (Billy Chapin) and Pearl (Sally Jane Bruce), escape from Powell in a rowboat, the cash hidden in Pearl's doll, while he pursues them across the Ohio

River Valley countryside. Film critic Edward Guthmann, writing for the *San Francisco Chronicle*, calls it "the film's greatest sequence, Pearl and John [floating] softly down a moonlit river, bound for an unseen providence. [Director Charles] Laughton and cinematographer Stanley Cortez film the children from the riverbank, placing a series of images — a frog, a spider's web, two rabbits — bodily in the foreground — surprisingly simple, a tad absurd, completely magical."

Eventually the kindly and elderly Rachel Cooper (the timeless Lillian Gish), who isn't hesitant about having both a gun and a bible, takes in the children, protecting them from the evil, murderous Powell.

Turning to David Thomson's book, *Biographical Dictionary of Films*, the noted film scholar says Mitchum "was one of the best actors in the movies. Since the war no American actor has made more first-class films, in so many different moods," which is exemplified in *The Night of the Hunter*, where he broke from his tough guy persona and "acted outside himself."

Mitchum has many extraordinary scenes in *The Night of the Hunter*, but the most unforgettable occurs when he tells the Harper children the story of left hand versus right hand. The words HATE and LOVE tattooed on the backs of his fingers, his eyes ablaze with madness, Mitchum's Powell proclaims: "Hate! It was with this left hand that the old brother Cain struck the blow that laid his brother low! And since that ungodly day, brethren, the left hand hath been the curse of almighty Jehovah."

Powell continues, "The right hand of Love.... The fingers of these hands, dear hearts—they're always a-tuggin' and a-warrin' one hand against the other.... Look at them, dear hearts. Old left hand Hate's a-fightin' and it looks like old Love's a goner. But wait now. Hot dog! Love's a-winning. Yesiree, old left hand Hate's a goner!"

A lesser actor would've overplayed the scene, but not Mitchum: He's in complete control of his acting—which is why his Reverend Powell is convincing and frightening.

CULT CLASSIC

Former Marine Danny Nardico was a good, crowd-pleasing light heavyweight, and his battle against equally tough Charley Norkus of Jersey City, on January 20, 1954, at the City Auditorium in Miami Beach, is considered a cult classic.

Entering the ring a five-to-one favorite, Nardico was looking forward to fighting heavyweight champion Rocky Marciano.

For the 2,535 in attendance at the City Auditorium in Miami Beach, it was a night to remember, and that's putting it mildly. Nardico was on the canvas six times and Norkus, who outweighed him by eighteen pounds, was decked twice. After Nardico went down in round nine, referee Jimmy Peerless stopped the fight.

Nardico had looked past Norkus, also a former Marine. A disastrous mistake.

Facts about Nardico:

1. His best punch, a left hook, dropped Jake LaMotta in the seventh round of their December 31, 1952, fight at the Coral Gables Coliseum in Florida. It marked the first time in his long career LaMotta had been knocked down. Nardico battered LaMotta savagely after the knockdown and his handlers refused to let the former middleweight champion come out for the eighth round. No mention of the knockdown and loss was made in Martin Scorsese's movie *Raging Bull* (1980), which earned Robert De Niro, playing LaMotta, an Oscar for Best Actor.

2. As an eighteen-year-old Marine, Nardico was a squad leader and saw action on Okinawa Shima, Ryukyu Island.

3. More important than Nardico's boxing career, which began in 1945 and ended with his retirement in 1956, was being awarded two Purple Hearts and a Silver Star.

Had Nardico defeated Norkus and fought Marciano, he would've been stopped early. Nardico's strategy of coming forward fearlessly and slugging it out was the only way he knew how to fight. Opponents who traded punches with Marciano didn't survive, because they were fighting his kind of fight.

Light-heavyweights, even the good ones, rarely have success against good heavyweights. Consider what happened to one of the best light-heavyweights of the 1950s, Harry "Kid" Matthews, when he fought Marciano.

Matthews was a genuine light-heavyweight unaccustomed to fighting heavyweights. Against fighters in his own weight class, he was practically unbeatable, compiling an 81-3-5 record, with 61 knockouts. A splendid boxer-puncher, he was a joy to watch, and among the fighters he had defeated were Irish Bob Murphy, Lloyd Marshall, and Nardico.

In 1952 he fought Marciano at Yankee Stadium, with the winner scheduled to fight heavyweight champion Jersey Joe Walcott. Weighing 182 to Marciano's 187, Matthews won the first round with his precise counterpunching.

In round two Marciano, undefeated in 40 fights, found the range. In his book about Marciano, *Unbeaten: Rocky Marciano's Fight for Perfection in a Crooked World*, Mike Stanton writes: "Chasing Matthews across the ring, Rocky hit him with a left jab, then two left hooks that 'damn near took his head off,' [Matthews's trainer George] Chemeres recalled."

It was the second hook that landed "flush on the jaw, [and] knocked [Matthews] down 'like a limp rag,' one writer said." As he struggled to get up, he fell back over the lower ring rope as referee Ray Miller counted him out.

After the loss to Marciano, Matthews fought thirteen times, winning nine, losing three, and fighting one draw. But he wasn't the same fighter he had been.

ELLEN'S AL

Al Pacino was the reason Ellen Barkin accepted the role of suspected serial killer Helen Cruger in Harold Becker's *Sea of Love* (1989). "'I would have said yes even if I never got chance to read the script,'" Andrew Yule quotes her as saying in *Life on the Wire: The Life and Art of Al Pacino.*

"'There are probably a handful of great actors around, and he is one of them. There's a lot to be learned from sitting across from Al for sixteen weeks on a set,' she said. 'There were many times when I had to ask him for help on this film, and he was right there.'"

Barkin tells Yule she complained to Becker that her character was "'supposed to be a mystery'" and there shouldn't be much known about her. "'You see her apartment and that she has a child. I tried to change that and make sure no one saw anything more about this woman than

[Pacino's Frank] Keller had when they were out on a date. But I lost that battle.'"

It's too bad Barkin lost the battle because making Cruger a mystery would've been a nice touch in a movie that's a mystery.

Pacino's Keller excels at his job, but he told Yule "'his dilemma interested me… because he is at a point in his life where he's being asked to retire and the job is all he has. [He has] no love interest in his life. He has his work, and you know there's work and there's love.'"

Fear of retiring clouded Keller's judgment and made him vulnerable, two reasons why he falls in love with Cruger, who's the number one suspect in several murders. If she's guilty she's a serial killer. She isn't guilty, however, which Keller learns in a violent showdown with the real killer near the end of the movie.

In the movie's last scene Keller, waiting outside for Cruger to appear after work, wins back her affection. A happy ending.

A better ending would've been this one: Cruger leaves the store where she works and Keller is standing patiently outside. Close up on Cruger. She sees Keller. Close up on Keller. He sees her. That's it! **THE END**.

BEST LEFT HOOK

When Joe Frazier was twelve years old, he fell on a rock and broke his left arm. Joe's father Rubin, Jerry Izenberg writes in *Once There Were Giants: The Golden Age of Heavyweight Boxing*, "barely etched a sharecropper's living out of the soil of his tiny [Beaufort, Alabama] acreage and couldn't afford a doctor." The arm healed by itself, which "may have been the reason Frazier had to work much harder than most other fighters to develop strength in that arm." It's why he possessed one of boxing's best left hooks.

When the Frazier family moved to Philadelphia, Joe, always interested in boxing, was discovered in the early nineteen-sixties by former boxer and World War II veteran Yank Durham, who guided him, as we know, to the world heavyweight championship in 1971.

Durham brought his undefeated power punching prospect along carefully. One of Frazier's opponents early in his career was cagey George "Scrap Iron" Johnson, a veteran heavyweight whose record was a middling 11-14-4. Johnson had battled such notables as Eddie Machen, Jerry Quarry, Elmer Rush, Thad Spencer, and Henry Clark.

Frazier couldn't knockout (or even knock down) Johnson, and though he won by decision, the Cloverlay people, who at this stage of Frazier's career sponsored him financially, were dissatisfied. The group believed Johnson should've been knocked out. Maybe Frazier wasn't as good as Durham said.

But Durham was pleased. "He had his guy in with a light-hitting opponent who couldn't hurt him," Izenberg writes, "but who, as a wise and older gym fighter, showed Frazier some things he hadn't seen before. It was the ultimate learning experience."

On March 8, 1971, at Madison Square Garden, Frazier became world heavyweight champion by decisioning a previously undefeated Muhammad Ali in what many boxing fans and historians have called the fight of the century.

And yes, I saw it. Not in person, but on the big screen at the fabled, smoke-filled New Haven Arena. An event, one not to be forgotten, and a far cry from the first professional boxing match I saw at the same New Haven Arena when I was eight or nine years old. Nathan Mann, a local heavyweight and pride of the city's Italian population, won a questionable decision over Bill Weinberg, which confused me because when Mann entered the ring he was cheered, but when he was declared the winner, the crowd booed him.

It was my introduction to a hometown decision.

From Mann and Weinberg to Frazier and Ali—so many years in between—certain things remained the same about the Arena, like the smoke. Blue and heavy. (Everybody smoked Camel cigarettes.)

That smoke! When I think about it, I still smell it.

JOLTIN' JOE, TEDDY BALLGAME, AND STAN THE MAN

Rather than put [the retired Ted] Williams in the press box with his old friends, the knights of the keyboard, the [New Yorker] magazine arranged for him to watch the game from a box seat.

Before one of the first games in Pittsburgh, a woman leaned over from an adjacent box and asked Williams to sign her souvenir program.

"You know, you're one of my favorite players," she said while he signed.

"Oh, is that right?" Williams replied.

"Yes," she said. And then she added, "I'm Stan Musial's mother."

According to Williams, he told her he ought to be asking for her *autograph.*

~George Vecsey,
Stan Musial: An American Life

Richard Ben Cramer's *Joe DiMaggio: The Hero's Life* is a biography of one of major league baseball's greatest all-around players. For DiMaggio's many fans, the book may be difficult to read because, pardon the cliché, it falls into the warts-and-all category.

Cramer's best writing is his coverage of the Yankee Clipper's 56 game hitting streak. It began May 15, 1941 and ended July 17.

A feat that will never be broken.

Some stats: In those 56 games, DiMaggio batted 223 times, hit safely 91 times, and walloped 15 homeruns. How many times did he whiff? Five times!

Connected to the streak is an intriguing story Cramer relates involving DiMaggio and an unnamed cab driver. It happened when he and Yankees pitcher Lefty Gomez were being driven to Cleveland's Municipal Stadium, and the cabbie boldly predicted if DiMaggio didn't get a hit his first time at bat, he wouldn't for the rest of the game and the streak would be over.

That night, Cleveland's starting pitcher was Al Smith. The first time DiMaggio stepped to the plate he hit a scorcher down the third baseline, but third baseman Ken Keltner made an exceptional play, threw to first base, and DiMaggio was out.

In Joe's last appearance at bat, Jim Bagby Jr. was Cleveland's pitcher and Joe, who had gone 0-for-2, grounded into a double play. The streak was over.

Joe's brother Dom played for the Boston Red Sox from 1940 to 1953. (He served in the military from 1943 to 1945). Nicknamed "The Little Professor," he was a seven-time All-Star. His lifetime major league batting average was .298.

When Dr. Rock Positano, in his memoir *Dinner with Di-Maggio: Memories of an American Hero,* co-written with his brother John, asked Joe if his brother Dom deserved to be inducted into Baseball's Hall of Fame, the Yankee Clipper's response was, "'Not bad, Doc, but not a great player.... He didn't have good enough seasons to be voted into the Hall of Fame.... Yeah, he was good, but Hall of Fame? No, he didn't earn it.'"

(Whoa! Didn't earn it? Come on, Joe.)

Joe's attitude about Dom might've been because the Boston centerfielder was, Positano points out, "a teammate and good friend of Joe's archrival Ted Williams...."

(Yes, Joe could be petty.)

For the many "Teddy Ballgame" fans out there, here's what "Joltin' Joe" tells Positano about Williams: "He and I were never the best of friends on or off the field, but he was a real war hero, a flyboy. He was a crack pilot, a fighting one, who locked wings with a fella named John Glenn.... Yeah, that John Glenn... the astronaut."

On the field Joe was baseball royalty — like Williams and Stan Musial. In retirement, he had problems adjusting to *not* being royalty. Also, he had an immigrant's suspicion of people. (Joe's parents were immigrants.)

George Vecsey, in his terrific book *Stan Musial: An American Life*, called Williams, Musial, and DiMaggio, all Hall of Famers, "The Big Three.... Musial was as close to a normal retired guy as a superstar can become, a frequent sight in the normal life of St. Louis.... Ted Williams mellowed, became accessible — goddamn right he did — talked hitting endlessly.... Joe DiMaggio was more of a hermit, trusting himself with a few close friends, hoarding golf bags he had cadged at celebrity outings."

And imagine this: Stan Musial playing baseball with either the New York Yankees, Brooklyn Dodgers, or New York Giants. Vecsey believes he would've been appreciated, but after a while one of those cities would've "demanded something more from him — more power, more championships, more quotes, more public visibility, some scandal, some controversy, something extra."

Vecsey continues: "He would have been scorned for not having Willie Mays's perceived glee (one of the great misconceptions of the sport), Joe DiMaggio's inscrutable hauteur, Mickey Mantle's self-destructiveness, or Duke Snider's brash sizzle. New York would have wanted more out of Musial. Not sure what — just more."

St. Louis was where Musial belonged!

One more thing. Nicknamed "Stan the Man" by Brooklyn fans, Musial terrorized the Dodgers during his career. In recognition of his talent old time, hard core Brooklynites — and they knew their baseball — voted him into the opponents' section of the Dodgers Hall of Fame.

THOSE DARN DOG DAYS

Cheer up, girls. You're going to be veterans of a bank robbery.

~*Al Pacino as Sonny*
Dog Day Afternoon

Al Pacino reminds me of a hockey player whose team is behind three or four goals and there's a minute remaining in the game. Though Pacino knows his team isn't going to win, he never stops giving his best, which is why his performances never disappoint.

Take an early Pacino movie, 1975's *Dog Day Afternoon*, which the great Sidney Lumet directed and is based on a true story. In a Best Actor nominated performance Pacino plays Sonny Wortzik, a Vietnam veteran whose behavior for the last year has alienated family and friends. One sweltering summer afternoon he and his friend Sal Naturale (John Cazale) decide to rob a Chase Manhattan Bank in Gravesend, Brooklyn.

The reason: Sonny needs money for his wife Leon's sex change operation. Enough said.

Turning to Frank Pierson's memorable dialogue, there's a scene early on when Mulvaney (Sully Boyar), the bank manager, tries to trip an alarm. Angered, Sonny, weapon in hand, bellows: "I'm a Catholic and I don't want to hurt anybody. Understand? No alarm!"

Then there's the head bank teller (Penelope Allen). Amazed at the ineptness of the two robbers, she blurts out, "Did you have a plan, or what? What did you do—just barge in on a whim? You don't have a plan. It's all whim."

"I got a plan," Sonny counters. "I had it planned. Only the money was supposed to be delivered, not taken away." (Sonny and Sal didn't know that earlier in the day the bank funds had been collected and not much money remained.)

Lastly, after the unarmed bank guard collapses, Mulvaney tells Sonny the man is asthmatic.

"He's got asthma—they make him a guard?" a bewildered Sonny says.

"He went to guard school," Mulvaney says.

Incredulous, Sonny asks, "To learn what? How to shoot? He doesn't even have a gun."

After FBI agent Sheldon (James Broderick) arrives, the movie's tone becomes serious. Sheldon emerges from his car and rudely ignores veteran Detective Sergeant Eugene Moretti (Charles Durning), who had been in charge of the attempted robbery investigation and with whom Sonny has established a rapport of sorts.

Later on, Moretti telephones headquarters and Sheldon, who's now in charge of the investigation, stands behind him. The detective barks, "Are you going to keep checkin' up on me?" and Sheldon arrogantly says, "Yeah," and walks away.

(Also, Sheldon takes credit for contacting Leon. A lie. Moretti did.)

Because of the duplicitous FBI agent's haughty behavior toward Moretti and the other police officers, we begin sympathizing with the inept Sonny. Clearly, the agent is too slick and shouldn't be trusted, but Sonny, naïve and desperate, trusts him. Mistake.

~~~

One of the movie's most poignant scenes belongs to Sonny's wife Leon (Chris Sarandon, in his movie debut). It's his telephone conversation with Sonny:

Leon: So, Sal's with you? Oh boy, you're better off giving up.

Sonny: I'm not going to give up because I've gone so far with this. Why should I give up now? I can't give up.

Leon: Would you do me a favor then?

Sonny: Yeah, what?

Leon: Well, these guys that have me down here. They think I'm a part of it. They think I'm a part of the plot to rob the bank.

Sonny: That's crazy, Leon. That's crazy. They're just…. They're just bullshitting you. They're giving you a snow job.

Leon: They told me I'm an accessory.

Sonny: No. That's just a con job on you, Leon. Don't listen to them.

Leon: What are you talkin'— I have to listen to them.

Sonny: No.

Leon: I can't survive in prison, Sonny.

Sonny: You're not going to prison. Nobody's going to prison.

Leon: How do you know?

Sonny: Because I know you're not going to prison, believe me.

Leon: Just tell 'em.

Sonny: Just tell 'em what? That you didn't do it? Are they on the phone there? (Shouting) Are they on the phone there?

Leon: Yeah.

Sonny: (Angry) That's great, you know. That's really terrific. You talk to me with them on the phone. That's really smart.

Leon: Well, I don't have a choice.

Sonny: What do you mean you didn't have a choice?

Leon: Well, what am I supposed to do? They're standing all around me. There are 7,000 fuckin' cops all around.

Name an emotion and Sarandon's distressed, confused Leon expresses it. A magnetic performance that earned him a well-deserved Best Supporting Actor nomination.

BANKS IS ON THE CASE

In Peter Robinson's second Detective Chief Inspector Alan Banks novel, *A Dedicated Man*, he's working in the fictional town of Eastvale, located near Yorkshire. Getting away from London, he thought, would make his job less stressful, less complicated. Wrong. He soon finds himself investigating the murder of a well-liked local man and the death of a teenage girl.

There are several suspects and crime fiction writer Jack Barker, whose hard-boiled novels are set in California, is one of them. (Shades of noir fiction master Raymond Chandler.)

Initially, Alan dislikes him because of his flippancy and "'well-practiced Clark Gable smile.'" Later he changes his mind. "'Barker's a clever bugger,' Banks says, 'but likable enough when you take the time to chat with him.'"

Another suspect is talented folksinger Penny Cartwright, who knew the dead man when she was a teenager.

In a scene with Cartwright—Banks no longer regards her as a suspect—she asks him if he's closing in on the murderer.

His response is key. He informs her of his method of "detection," which, he stresses, is "'not a matter of getting closer like a zoom lens, but of getting enough bits and pieces to transform chaos into a recognizable pattern....You can't predict when that moment will come. It could be in the next ten seconds or the next ten years. You don't know what the pattern will look like when it's there, so you might not even recognize it at first. But soon enough, you'll know you've got a design."

A thought-provoking character is Superintendent Gristhorpe. Introduced to readers in Robinson's first novel, he's a big man, standing well over six feet. It's his "eyes," Robinson writes, "[that] had been known to draw out confessions from even the hardest of villains and had made many an underling, caught out in a manufactured statement of an overenthusiastic interrogation, blush and hide in shame." His "eyes shone with a gentle love of life and a sense of compassion that would have given the Buddha himself a good run for his money."

Also, he hungers for literary classics. His home bookcase is stocked with the works of Homer, Dante, Wordsworth, Dickens, Joyce, and Austen, and in his Eastvale office, Robinson writes, "books [are] everywhere, and not all of them relevant to police work."

CALL HIM WILL

Anthony, Ophelia, and Norrie

In Anthony Burgess's book *Shakespeare*, the author fittingly refers to William Shakespeare as WILL. "We would not want to call Milton Jack," Burgess writes, "but Shakespeare seems to ask for an intimacy of address."

That said, take the chapter titled "School," which is where Burgess addresses those people who refuse to believe Shakespeare was the author of all those immortal comedies and dramas.

Their reasoning is that there's no way the son of illiterate parents could write such works. Burgess believes they're wrong. And they are! "It is nonsense to suppose that high art needs high learning," Burgess writes. "Any peasant can teach himself to write and write well. Any peasant writer can, by reading the appropriate books and by keeping his senses alert, give the illusion of great knowledge of the world."

He continues: "What no amount of academic training can bestow on a potential writer is the gift of words. The artist does not have to be a courtier, traveler, or scholar, though it may be his task to create such men out of his imagination."

Moving to the tragedy *Hamlet* and specifically to Ophelia, Hamlet's girlfriend who drowns herself "amid crow flowers, nettles, daisies." Queen Gertrude, Hamlet's mother, describes Ophelia's death to Laertes, the young woman's brother: **"Her clothes spread wide, / And mermaid-like awhile they bore her up, / Which time she chanted snatches of old lauds, / As one incapable of her own distress /...But long it could not be / Till that her garments, heavy with their drink, / Pulled the poor wretch from her melodious lay / To muddy death."**

In her book *The Friendly Shakespeare*, Norrie Epstein is spot-on when she writes that Ophelia is the drama's most sympathetic character: "At her first appearance we see an innocent, trusting, and spirited young girl but by the last scene she is contaminated, mad, and knowing.... Shakespeare gives her one of the most cryptic lines in the play: 'Lord, we know what we are, but know not what we may be.' Ophelia goes mad because she discovers what others 'may be.' Tragically, she never learns what she might have become."

Her father Polonius, Epstein continues, "exhibits no tenderness toward his daughter. He's interested in her only as a source of information to pass along to Claudius, and thus make himself politically useful. His indelicate language and cruel insinuations poison her mind with the smut, spying, and sexual innuendo that infect the Danish court. Hamlet then abuses and deserts her, believing that she, along with his mother, has betrayed him."

Ophelia goes insane, Epstein writes, "After [Hamlet] has killed her father...."

Mr. Tisdale

In the early nineteen-sixties I took a wonderful evening course in Shakespeare, at what was then New Haven State Teachers College. Taught by a Yale graduate student — his name was William Tisdale — our first reading assignment was *Hamlet*, then write a short paper about the tragedy's most sympathetic character.

My pick was Hamlet because I felt sorry for the young guy: His mother, after her husband's death, married her brother-in-law Claudius. They hooked up so quickly that "The funeral bak'd meats/ Did furnish forth the marriage tables."

(Hamlet learns Claudius murdered his father — with Gertrude's approval — and is now King of Denmark. Needless to say, but I'll say it anyway, Claudius and Gertrude hope to live happily ever after. Hamlet has, however, quite a bit to say about their union.)

Anyway, I notched a B on the paper — which I typed on a portable Royal — along with some encouraging comments from Mr. T.

The instructor brought Shakespeare to life. He did it with great enthusiasm — which taught me that in the world of education, public or otherwise, the best teachers and school administrators are enthusiastic about their work.

"An enthusiast is willing to go to any trouble to impart the glad news bubbling within him," H.L. Mencken writes in *Prejudices*. "[The teacher] thinks that [the subject] is important and valuable to know; given the slightest glow of interest in a pupil to start with, he will fan that glow to a flame. No hollow formalism cripples him and slows him down."

Many years later I bought Epstein's book, which was published in 1993, and she was right about Ophelia being the tragedy's most sympathetic creation.

Lesson learned from Ms. Epstein: Pay attention to supporting characters.

A WINK DID IT

Audrey Hepburn appeared in seven movies, though never as the lead, before costarring in William Wyler's *Roman Holiday* (1953). It was her breakthrough film and her performance earned her the year's Oscar for Best Actress.

In the movie Hepburn's British Princess Ann bucks royalty by escaping from her embassy to experience life in Rome. There she meets a reporter, the streetwise Joe Bradley (Gregory Peck). After Joe learns she's a princess, he feigns ignorance about her true identity: He's after a story. An exclusive!

Predictably, he and Princess Ann fall in love.

A classic American romantic, escapist comedy, the movie holds up well because charm is one of its main ingredients—and charm is timeless.

According to Diana Maychick in *Audrey Hepburn: An Intimate Portrait*, Wyler spotted Hepburn in 1951's *Laughter in Paradise*. Maychick quotes him as saying, "'She looked completely the part of a princess. A real, live, bona fide princess. And when she opened her mouth, you were sure you'd found a princess.'" The big question was: "'Could she act like a princess?'"

At one point during her audition for *Roman Holiday*, Hepburn thought the camera had stopped filming. But it hadn't. "She was seated on a bed for the scene," Maychick writes, "and when she jumped off of it, she winked." For the people who saw the audition, "Audrey won the role of Princess Ann in that brief moment, exuding charm and playfulness and a regard for propriety."

The most memorable scene in the movie occurs when Hepburn doesn't act—and it works. "Joe and the princess encounter a wall bearing an ancient sculpted face with an open mouth," Gary Fishgall explains in *Gregory Peck: A Biography*. "The reporter dares her to stick her hand in the opening, warning her that, according to legend, the creature will bite off the hand of anyone who is lying. Since neither he nor she has been completely honest with the other, the prospect is intimidating."

Peck's character goes first, but before filming the scene the actor "suggested to Wyler that he keep the gag going by pulling his arm out with his hand hidden in the sleeve of his suit jacket."

Wyler loved the idea but told Peck not to tell Hepburn.

Fishgall quotes Peck: "'Keeping her in the dark is what made the scene work.... Her startled look of surprise leaps off the screen. She screams then dissolves into laughter. It is one of the most candid and indelible moments of *Roman Holiday.'"*

PISSED OFF PAT

There must be readers out there who agree with what Bradley Cooper's Pat Solitano, in the film *The Silver Linings Playbook* (2012), says about Ernest Hemingway's novel *A Farewell to Arms* and its two main characters, Lt. Frederic Henry, an ambulance driver in Italy during World War I, and Catherine Barkley, a brave, admirable English nurse with whom he has fallen in love.

I'll be more specific: It's the way Hemingway ended his novel that sent Pat into a tizzy.

Here's what happened: At home one evening, the thirty-year-old Pat, who had been institutionalized in a Baltimore mental health facility, barges into his parents' bedroom after reading Hemingway's novel and begins ranting about Catherine being pregnant and she and Lt. Henry are "going to be happy. Isn't that wonderful? She's pregnant and they escape into the mountains and they're going to be happy and they're going to be drinking wine and they dance with each other. There's a scene of them dancing, which is boring, but I liked it because they were happy. Do you think he ends it there? No! He writes another ending. She dies, Dad. I mean, the world's hard enough as it is, guys. It's fucking hard enough as it is. Can't somebody say 'hey let's be positive, let's have a good ending to the story?'"

It's clear the edition of the novel Pat didn't read was *The Hemingway Library Edition of A Farewell to Arms* (Scribner,2012), which includes in its appendix forty-seven alternative endings. Maybe he would've been satisfied with one of them.

I'll set the stage for the ending Hemingway used in his novel: Catherine has died in the hospital delivery room and so has their baby boy. (From a doctor, Lt. Henry learns Catherine "had one hemorrhage after another. They couldn't stop it." Later, a nurse informs him the boy was stillborn.)

Here's Hemingway's published ending: "But after I had got [the nurses] out and shut the door and turned off the light it wasn't any good," Lt. Henry says. "It was like saying goodbye to a statue. After a while I went on out and left the hospital and walked back to the hotel in the rain."

Sure, Pat, you're right. Very sad. No argument there.

Directed by David O. Russell, *The Silver Linings Playbook* movie was adapted from Matthew Quick's novel. Like the movie, Quick's book is set in Collingswood, New Jersey, and we soon learn there's another book, not only

Hemingway's, that frustrates Pat. It's F. Scott Fitzgerald's *The Great Gatsby*.

After reading it, Pat says, "I feel like ripping the book in half and calling up Fitzgerald and telling him his book is all wrong, even though I know Fitzgerald is probably deceased… you can tell Fitzgerald never took the time to look up at clouds during sunset, because there's no silver lining at the end of the book, let me tell you."

There are a few things I'd say to Pat, were I to meet him, and one of them is: "Listen to me, young man. Calm down! So what if Hemingway's and Fitzgerald's characters didn't reach the silver lining? Lt. Frederick Henry, Catherine Barkley, Jay Gatsby, Nick Carraway — they're characters in a novel. OK? Believe me, Pat, they're not real."

But the truth is Pat isn't real either, which means, I guess, I really can't say anything to him.

JACK'S HOBOING

Jack Kerouac's *On the Road* is an American classic that has almost eclipsed his other writings, like his 1960 book of essays *Lonesome Traveler*. The book is, in part, written in what Kerouac called spontaneous prose.

And Kerouac's spontaneous prose violates almost every rule of traditional writing. For example, some sentences don't end with periods but are connected with commas. (How ghastly!) Other sentences run into each other without any punctuation. (Naughty! Naughty!) Parenthesis? Well, they're used as if they're pals: **( ) ( )**. The dash? Often Kerouac uses it to begin sentences.

One of Kerouac's critics is Truman Capote, who condemns his writing style as "just typing."

But hold on! The secret weapon Kerouac's admirers have is what Benjamin Dreyer writes in his book *Dreyer's English*. Maybe Dreyer had Kerouac in mind when he says,

142

" ...artistry, however you want to define that slippery concept, can outrank and outweigh notions of what might conventionally be deemed 'correct'; where voice—eccentric, particular, peculiar as it may be—is paramount."

Here's a suggestion, reader: Frustrating as Kerouac's writing style may be, stay with it because you'll discover in his works such sage gems as these:

"The best teacher is experience and not through someone's distorted point of view"

" ...a sociable smile is nothing but a mouth full of teeth."

"Paris is a woman but London is an independent man puffing his pipe in a pub."

"It's only through form that we can realize emptiness."

"So love life for what it is, and form no preconceptions whatever in your mind."

This brings me to "The Vanishing American Hobo," *Lonesome Traveler*'s final essay, which begins this way: "The American hobo has a hard time hoboing nowadays due to the increase in public surveillance of highways, railroad yards, sea shores, river bottoms, embankments, and the thousand and one hiding holes of industrial night."

A hobo becomes a bum when he loses his pride and finds himself on skid row. "There he sleeps in the doorway, back to the wall, head down," Kerouac writes, "with his right hand palm-up as if to receive from the night, the other hand hanging, strong, firm, like Joe Louis hands," but "made tragic by unavoidable circumstance...."

It's as if the "poor bum of the skid row [is saying] 'I've had enough, I give up, I quit....'"

In 1956, while living in Tucson, Arizona, Kerouac lived as a hobo. One morning, at 2 A.M., he was stopped by police and questioned.

"I just spent a summer with the Forest Service," Kerouac tells the officer. Asked if he was paid for his work, he says that he was. The officer responds, "Then why don't you go to a hotel?" Kerouac's answer: "I like it better outdoors [because] I'm studying hobo." The officer asks, "What's so good about that?" and then, "Go ahead if that's what you want."

Jack isn't taken into custody because "I was sincere with them and they ended up scratching their heads."

My favorite passage in *Lonesome Traveler* appears in the chapter titled "Alone on a Mountaintop." That's where Kerouac's writing becomes visionary, one of his greatest strengths as a writer.

We read: "And it seemed as I sat there that this was the Primordial Bear and that he owned all the Northwest and all the snow and commanded all the mountains. — He was King Bear, who could crush my head in his paws... and this was his house, his yard, his domain... he prowled at night among unknown lakes, and in the early morning the pearl-pure light that shadowed mountainsides of fir made him blink with respect. —He had millenniums of prowling here behind him... and would see much more... he was aware of the light material the world is made of, yet he never discoursed, nor communicated by signs, nor wasted a breath complaining —he just nibbled and pawed and lumbered along snags paying no attention to things inanimate or animate...."

Kerouac knows what will happen next: "Soon he would come out of the fog, huge, and come and stare in my window with his big burning eyes. —He was Avalokitesvara* the Bear, and his sign was the gray wind of autumn.

—"I was waiting for him. He never came."

*In *Dharma Bums*, Kerouac defines Avaloki-tesvara as "the Hearer and Answerer of Prayer."

BIBLIOGRAPHY

Books

Burgess, Anthony. *Shakespeare*

Camus, Albert. *Resistance, Rebellion, and Death*

Cannon, Jimmy. *Nobody Asked Me But...The World of Jimmy Cannon*

Carroll, Lewis. *Alice's Adventures in Wonderland*

Carroll, Lewis. *The Hunting of the Snark: An Agony in Eight Fits*

Churchill, Winston S. *The Early Years: 1879-1904*

Cramer, Ben. *Joe DiMaggio: The Hero's Life*

Danielewski, Mark Z. *House and Leaves*

Douglas, Kirk. *The Ragman's Son*

Dreyer, Benjamin. *Dreyer's English: An Utterly Correct Guide to Clarity and Style*

Eliot, Marc. *American Titan: Searching for John Wayne*

Epstein, Lorrie. *The Friendly Shakespeare*

Fishgall, Gary. *Gregory Peck: A Biography*

Fitch, Jerry. *James Louis Bivins: The Man Who Would be Champion*

Fitzgerald, F. Scott. *The Great Gatsby*

Grobel, Lawrence. *Al Pacino in Conversation with Lawrence Grobel*

Heinz, W.C. *Once They Heard the Cheers*

Hemingway, Ernest. *A Farewell to Arms*

Hemingway, Ernest. *A Moveable Feast*

Horowitz, Anthony. *The House of Silk*

Izenberg, Jerry. *Once There Were Giants: The Golden Age of Heavyweight Boxing*

Kerouac, Jack. *Dharma Bums*

Kerouac, Jack. *Lonesome Traveler*

Kimball, George. *Four Kings: Leonard, Hagler, Hearns, and Duran and the Last Great Era of Boxing*

Kinsella, W.P. *Shoeless Joe*

Krutch, Joseph Wood. *The Forgotten Peninsula*

Le Guin, Ursula. *No Time to Spare: Thinking about What Matters*

Maltin, Leonard. *Leonard Maltin's Movie Encyclopedia*

Matchick, Diana. *Audrey Hepburn: An Intimate Portrait*

Maynard, Candice. *Hero of the Empire: The Boer War, a Daring Escape, and the Making of Winston Churchill*

McCarten, Anthony. *Darkest Hour*

Melville, Herman. *Moby Dick*

Mencken, H.L. *Prejudices*

Miller, Arthur. *A View from the Bridge*

Oates, Joyce Carol. *On Boxing*

Pep, Willie (with Robert Sacchi). *Willie Pep Remembers... Friday's Heroes*

Positano, Dr. Rock (with John Positano). *Dinner with DiMaggio: Memories of An American Hero*

Prejean, Sister Helen. *Dead Man Walking*

Robinson, Peter. *A Dedicated Man*

Sculthorpe, Derek. *Van Heflin: A Life in Film*

Shakespeare, William. *Hamlet*

Stanton, Mike. *Unbeaten: Rocky Marciano's Fight for Perfection in a Crooked World*

Thomson, David. *Biographical Dictionary of Films*

Toledo, Springs. *Murderers' Row*

Toledo, Springs. *Smokestack Lightning*

Vecsey, George. *Stan Musial: An American Life*

Williams, Dave (with James Lawton). *Tiger – A Hockey Story*

Winters, Shelley. *Also Known as Shirley*

Yule, Andrew. *Life on the Wire: The Life and Art of Al Pacino*

Zinsser, William. *On Writing Well: An Informal Guide to Nonfiction*

Movies and DVDs

Act of Violence (1949)

Alibi (DVD/2008)

Detective Story (1949)

Dial M for Murder (1954)

Doc Martin (2016/DVD)

Dog Day Afternoon (1975)

Foyle's War (2002/DVD)

Heat (1995)

He Ran All the Way (1951)

Looking for Richard (1996)

Roman Holiday (1953)

Sea of Love (1989)

The Night of the Hunter (1955)

The Silver Linings Playbook (2012)

Magazines and Newspapers

Garner, Jack. *Gannett News Service.* (date unavailable)

Bond, Gwenda. *Salon* (date unavailable)

Collis, Clark. *Entertainment Weekly* (date unavailable)

Guthmann, Edward. *San Francisco Chronicle* (date unavailable)

The Week (May 25, 2018)

The International Boxing Research Journal (Issue 140/ December 2018)

The International Research Journal (December 2017)

ABOUT THE AUTHOR

Roger Zotti was born in New Haven, CT, graduated from Eastern Connecticut State College in 1966, and received his master's degree from Wesleyan University in 1971.

He taught adult education at a Connecticut Correctional Center for over twenty years, retiring in 1993. A regular contributor to the *International Boxing Research Organization Journal* and *The Resident*, a Connecticut newspaper, he also facilitates a movie class for Adventures in Lifelong Learning in Norwich, CT, and is a member of the Connecticut Boxing Hall of Fame Induction Committee.

Hockey, running, women's basketball, boxing, movies (old and new), reading, and music are some of his interests.

He and his wife, Maryann, live in Preston, CT, along with their adventurous dog. They have two adult children, Thomas and Leslie.

www.ingramcontent.com/pod-product-compliance
Lightning Source LLC
Chambersburg PA
CBHW071248210626
46818CB00013B/490